Absent Fathers, Lost Sons

A C.G. JUNG FOUNDATION BOOK

The C. G. Jung Foundation for Analytical Psychology is dedicated to helping men and women grow in conscious awareness of the psychological realities in themselves and society, find healing and meaning in their lives and greater depth in their relationships, and live in response to their discovered sense of purpose. It welcomes the public to attend its lectures, seminars, films, symposia, and workshops and offers a wide selection of books for sale through its bookstore. The Foundation also publishes *Quadrant,* a semiannual journal, and books on Analytical Psychology and related subjects. For information about Foundation programs or membership, please write to the C. G. Jung Foundation, 28 East 39th Street, New York, NY 10016.

Absent FATHERS, Lost SONS

The Search For Masculine Identity

GUY CORNEAU

Translated by Larry Shouldice

SHAMBHALA
Boston & London
1991

Shambhala Publications, Inc.
Horticultural Hall
300 Massachusetts Avenue
Boston, Massachusetts 02115

9   8   7   6

Printed in the United States of America on acid-free
paper ♾

Design by Diane Levy

Distributed in the United States by Random House,
Inc., and in Canada by Random House of Canada Ltd

Library of Congress Cataloging-in-Publication Data

Corneau, Guy.
    [Père manquant, fils manqué. English]
    Absent fathers, lost sons: the search for
masculine identity/Guy Corneau; translated by
Larry Shouldice.—1st ed.
        p.   cm.
    Translation of: Père manquant, fils manqué.
    "A C. G. Jung Foundation book."
    Includes bibliographical references.
    ISBN 0-87773-603-0
    1. Men—Psychology.   2. Masculinity
(Psychology)   3. Fathers and sons.   I. Title.
HQ1090.C6713   1991   90-53373
306.874′2—dc20   CIP

For my father, Alcide,
and for my friends
François, Robert, and Louis
for their loyalty

CONTENTS

ACKNOWLEDGMENTS

Above all others, I wish to thank the men and women, my friends and patients, who gave me permission to use what is usually referred to in the business as their "case material." This material, which is actually their most intimate words, has provided the substance for this book. I present their words with respect, in the hope that they can help other men and women.

I am also very grateful to my friend Nathalie Coupal for her patient revision of the manuscript and her statistical research; her work was truly admirable. I would like to thank Joane Boucher for typing the initial version of the book, Jean Grondin for subsequent versions, and Jany Hogue for her suggestions regarding style. The first men and women to read the book, Nicole Plamondon, François Bruneau, and Gilbert David, were most important; their judicious advice enabled me to rein in my enthusiasm and let the book mature. I would also like to express my appreciation to my colleagues Jan Bauer and Tom Kelly for their repeated encouragement.

My thanks also to my editors at the Editions de l'Homme, which published the original French version: Bernard Prévost, who first suggested this book, and Jean Bernier, who followed it through the various stages in its evolution. I very much appreciate their tact and intelligence.

I am grateful to Larry Shouldice, who patiently and skillfully translated this book into English. Working with him, I came to realize that translation is not simply a technical process, but a labor of love involving words and language. I also thank Judith Larin for her diligent reading of the English text, and I should mention Tom Kelly again, for his supervision of the whole translation process.

I am indebted to Aryeh Maidenbaum, Director of the C. G. Jung Foundation in New York for his enthusiastic support of my work in male psychology. Finally, I am deeply grateful to the team at Shambhala Publications, in particular to Jonathan Green and David O'Neal, for their kindness and openness.

Without the love of all these people, this book would have remained a prisoner of silence.

Absent Fathers, Lost Sons

INTRODUCTION

Appearing before a parliamentary commission on mental
health issues, Hubert Wallot, a physician and professor at the
University of Quebec at Chicoutimi, recently expressed his
concern that no government has established a council on the
status of men. With the support of statistical evidence, he
undertook to illustrate the precarious condition of men's
general health:

> *During their childhood and adolescence, men are more likely
> [than women] to suffer from slow mental development, a short
> attention span due to "hyperactivity," behavioral problems,
> "hyperanxiety," schizoid difficulties, transient or chronic
> spasms, stuttering, functional enuresis and encopresis [invol-
> untary urination and defecation], sleepwalking and night-
> mares, autism, as well as persistent and specific developmental
> problems such as dyslexia.*
>
> *As adults, men make up a significant percentage of those
> who present personality disorders related to paranoia and
> compulsive or antisocial behavior (as evidenced by the large
> number of them in prisons). Men also far outnumber women
> in the frequency of transexuality and sexual perversions.*[1]

---

1. Huguette O'Neil, "Santé mentale: les hommes, ces grands oubliés . . ."
("Mental Health: Men, the Forgotten Group . . ."), *L'Actualité médicale*, 11
May 1988, p. 27 (parentheses added).

Dr. Wallot notes that four times as many men suffer from alcoholism and drug addiction as do women; they also outnumber women three to one in the areas of suicide and high-risk behavior. In addition, men are more prone than women to schizophrenia. Dr. Wallot concludes that *the frequent absence of the father or of masculine models for young male children "seems to explain certain behavioral difficulties connected with men's affirmation of their sexual identity."*[2]

In short this implies that, in spite of their seemingly independent nature, many men are looking for their fathers—and many of them are in need of help. I have seen for myself how great their need is, how anxious they are to get together and discuss it. In the spring of 1987, after giving a lecture entitled "The Fear of Intimacy and Repressed Aggressivity in Men," I decided to organize a one-day workshop for a group of men. On Saturday morning there were twenty-one of them waiting for me in the hall of the Jung Center in Montreal. These included fathers, married and divorced men, bachelors, gay men, a punk, a cook, a decorator, an accountant, artists, welfare recipients, therapists, civil servants, and teachers; they ranged in age from twenty to fifty. It turned out to be an amazing experience, a day filled with utterly astonishing confessions and revelations. When it came to an end, all the participants decided to continue meeting and working together on a regular basis.

In response to my first question, "Do you feel like a man?," not one of them answered in the affirmative, not even the older ones who had been married for twenty years, or the ones who had children. It quickly became apparent that our sense of identity does not necessarily correspond to our life experiences, but rather to our inner sense of a solid foundation or its lack.

This lack of foundation in the lives of men today is what I want to talk about in this book. I want to talk about the

---

2. Quoted in ibid.

feelings of misery these men expressed in the group sessions and the problems other men confessed to when they were alone with me in my office. I also want to talk about the things we began to open up and explore together, especially the fragility of masculine identity.

This fragility is perhaps reflected in the fact that, fairly typically, men today decide to have their first child at the age of thirty-five or forty, which is a good deal later in life than they had started families in previous generations. Could it be that this time lag is a measure of the number of years men now need to consolidate their own identity? This seems to me to be the case, even though a lot of other factors also come into play for these children of the postwar baby boom: a greater degree of individualism, more physical comfort, an increase in stress, the incredible proliferation of technological innovations, and, of course, a terrible sense of uncertainty about the future of our planet. It is interesting to look at these questions from an exclusively psychological point of view, though, and this is what I propose to do.

The raw material for this book comes from clinical observations in my practice as an analyst. All the cases have been disguised, except in their essential details, and the material has been used only with the consent of the individuals involved. Also, it should be kept in mind that my examples and my interpretations deal with only one facet of a person, so only one fragment of the individual's personality is presented in each instance. It would be a mistake, then, to dramatize the cases in question by either oversimplifying them or to make excessive generalizations based on material that is necessarily incomplete. In several instances I have created fictitious characters by combining the experiences of several different people.

My discussion is also based on symbolic images of dreams and on images from the unconscious, which always add richness and variety to our observations. These images have the great advantage of providing a less abstract basis for the investigation of any particular theme, and they address the world of emotions directly. As Jung said, nothing is less scientific than the analysis of dreams; their relevance, however, makes an impression on our minds and sets us to thinking about the unknown that lies within each of us. After all, is it not by imagining a thing intensely, by trying to fit an image to an emotion, and by letting our most secret fantasies rise to the surface, that we can most effectively understand the nature of psychological phenomena? Is this not how we objectify these phenomena in order to dialogue with them? Mythological stories play the same role as these images: they put our contemporary experiences into perspective by revealing the ways in which our experiences are eternally human.

This book is a synthesis of what I have read, seen, heard, and felt about men in the past three years, and of what I have felt about my own life as a man. I do not claim that the ideas developed here are in any way full or complete. Making such a claim is not my goal, and in any case I do not insist on being "right." In point of fact, I deal only with those themes that grip me from within.

The question of the father and masculine identity surges up into our contemporary world from the depths of the collective unconscious. The best we can do is consider the question and try to remain open to new developments as they evolve. The images that inhabit us propel us toward the future. I do not know what a man is, and know even less what a man should be. Rather I try to feel what he is and to get to know him from the inside. I try to let the man within myself emerge into the light.

There is no perfect model for man, just as there is no perfect family. We are all the products of a more or less inadequate past that pushes us forward and forces us to adapt creatively. Many of our parents had to struggle to secure their material necessities, and so their consciousness is largely defined by their need to assure their physical survival. They speak only through their actions, unable to give verbal expression to their love or their disappointments. They have trouble disengaging their individuality from their function as father and mother, and they feel awkward about expressing their inner feelings.

Through the window of our own awareness we can glimpse a world so different from theirs that any chance of a dialogue with them seems impossible. This is because the frames of our windows are psychological, and we view the world through them as a network of psychological relations. We should not forget, however, that the very education and material security made possible by our parents enable us to respond to the internal needs that concern us today.

It is not fathers and mothers that I judge in this book—it is the silence that envelops us all. The role of sons, now, is to break through this silence finally. The soul of the world always goes into hiding wherever there is trouble and disorder; this hidden soul is tormenting men today. More than ever before, we are sitting in the hot seat of change.

ONE

The Absent Father

Psychoanalysts must probe the imagination; whether one conceives of an imaginary father, a symbolic father, or a real father (keeping in mind that the real does not exist), the profusion of signifiers associated with the father hides one important fact: these father *signifiers are* empty.[1]

Christiane Olivier

THE FATHER'S SILENCE

I had barely begun writing this chapter when I remembered a dream I had the night before:

I have to help a sexy, dark-haired, dynamic Jane Fonda get a portly old gentleman up to the second floor of the building next door so that he can go to the bathroom. When we start climbing the stairs the man stands directly behind me and grabs on to my belt. He does nothing to help, so the climb is extremely difficult: I literally have to drag him behind me. I

---

1. Christiane Olivier, "Pères empêchés" ("Thwarted Fathers"), *Autrement* (Pères et fils), no. 16, Paris, June 1984, p. 205.

feel his full weight pulling at me, and my belt, stretched to the breaking point, digs painfully into my body.

Reappearing as it did, just as I was about to begin writing, this dream started me thinking about how difficult it is to confront the past: to drag the old man, who symbolizes it, to a place where he can get relief. How the past weighs me down and cuts into my body! How heavy it is to lift my experiences with my own father into the realm of consciousness! Luckily Jane Fonda is there to help me: this really is a workout! In the dream she is actually the one I'm doing it for; it is as if my anima,[2] in the form of an actress, an expert at expressing emotions, is demanding an end to the silence I have inherited.

So many things rose back to the surface with this dream: the good and bad moments of my relationship with my father. I remembered the games we used to play, the way we used to team up against my mother. I also remembered his stories about growing up in the woods, his poor but happy childhood, the years he worked as a lumberjack, his move to the city. These stories had become real myths for me, myths that I never tired of hearing. Then suddenly, when I entered puberty, when I needed him most, he was no longer there. He had disappeared, vanished.

In actual fact, I was the one who disappeared, when I went off to boarding school at the seminary. At the beginning I got out of there for only four hours a week to see my family. I remember how every Sunday I hoped we'd have some sort of conversation, my father and I. I used to sit in my mother's armchair, beside the one my father sat in, reading his paper. I wanted so much for him to say something to me, talk to me, tell me whatever he wanted to: things about his work, rockets

---

2. For Jung the anima represents the feminine part of a man, just as the animus represents the masculine part of a woman. The anima or animus is in fact the sexual opposite that everyone carries within, since sex is determined by a single chromosome. The anima is a man's internal, unconscious personality, the bridge that connects him to the inner world.

and spaceships, anything. I kept trying to come up with questions that might interest him. Desperately needing him to recognize me, I played "the man." It never worked. Maybe I simply didn't interest him, or maybe he felt he had already done his duty. After all, it was he who had made possible for me the education that had been denied him.

Later, when I was reaching the end of my education (and while my father was suffering from his own lack of education), we did attempt a few conversations, but they always led to dead ends. The way he defended his positions left no room for mine; at least that was how I perceived it. Again my father left me alone, refusing to recognize me; my arguments were worthless and always would be. I could try, but I was not a man. If only he could have known how hard I was trying to reach him, how much I needed him! If only I could have told him.

Although I was very young at the time, I still remember how, when my father's brothers would come to visit, he would spend the whole afternoon with them down in the basement, talking about everything from God to the meaning of life. Perched at the top of the stairs, listening to the echoes of their conversations, I was entranced; I couldn't wait to be a grownup so I'd be able to take part in the discussions too. Then when I did grow up, though, my father was afraid of discussing things with me because my values were too different from his. All he did was elicit my guilt with his silence. I sat there in my mother's chair, waiting for my father to speak. I felt timid, tongue-tied; I was begging for confirmation of my manhood. My father's silence, though, commanded me to remain always a little boy, in awe of his reserve—which I mistook for strength.

These fragments are all part of a story that can hardly be called tragic: after all, I had a father who was more present than the fathers of most teenagers at that time. Telling this story still causes me pain, though. To this very day, whenever I want to talk seriously with my father, I still feel tongue-tied.

A heaviness comes over me, an invisible barrier that seems terribly difficult to get past. It is as though it were somehow taboo to speak to him. The barrier definitely remains, despite our good intentions; the only difference is that now I feel I'm as responsible for it as he is. I love my father, but I don't know how to break down the wall between us. At times even wanting to break it down seems almost indecent. What can it be that I am so frightened of?

The Law of Silence

Through my lectures and my practice as an analyst, I have learned that the pain I feel is shared by many others. All men live more or less in a hereditary silence that has been passed down from generation to generation, a silence that denies every teenage boy's need for recognition—or confirmation—from his father. It is almost as though our fathers are subject to a rule of silence that decrees that fathers who speak are a threat to male solidarity.

Our fathers fled into the woods or the taverns or their work. They sought refuge in their cars, newspapers, TV programs. Often they chose to escape into an abstract, synthetic world, a world apart from present reality, from everyday experience, from their own bodies. In the past and in the present, men have succumbed to the powerful seduction of the mass media, that sings to them like the mermaids who would have lured Ulysses onto the rocks. Men's dependence on the media, like a drug addiction, lets them avoid speaking, avoid inhabiting their bodies, avoid entering into relationships. The pseudo-independence of men is really no more than a subtle form of self-absorption.

Actually, we can't put all the blame on our fathers, since they themselves are victims of history. Obviously we are far removed today from the ecological niche that allowed young males of our species regular access to their fathers, in order to observe how the fathers went about things. Contemporary men in fact find few occasions to experience or actualize their masculine potential in the presence of their fathers. Since the beginning of the industrial era, there has been less and less prolonged contact between fathers and sons. A distortion seems to have crept in between the innate needs of sons and the behavior of present-day fathers, who appear as pitiful figures, trapped in a fate over which they are powerless. Fathers feel increasingly caught in a vacuum as ancestral habits continue to fall away, and this contributes more and more to the breakdown of masculine identity.

"My God, Why Hast Thou Forsaken Me?"

Myths reveal to us the basic structures of history; the silence of the father and the suffering of the son have been heralded in the Christian myth. This central myth that has guided the last two centuries of our evolution is marked to an astonishing degree by the absence of the father. Saint Joseph's paternity was called into question from the very beginning, and he participated very little in the active life of his son Jesus. He was not there at the foot of the cross with Mary and the Apostles; it was not Joseph but Mary, holding her dead son in her arms, that Michelangelo immortalized in his *Pietà*. The words of Christ on the Cross could hardly have been more explicit: "My God, my God, why hast thou forsaken me?"

The Absent Father

In a more immediate sense, if we look at the statistics dealing with fathers who are physically absent from the home, we find that the problem of absent fathers is extremely widespread. In the United States, for example, one in five children lives in a fatherless home. In fact, it is estimated that one of every four children lives in a single-parent family and that 89 percent of these families are headed by women.[3]

In Canada, according to the 1986 census almost one child

---

3. This statistic was reported on the Radio-Canada television news program "Le Point," April 4, 1988.

in seven lives in a fatherless family. One of every five families (18.8 percent) has only one parent, and of these single-parent families, 79 percent are headed by single women. In other words, single-parent families account for 16 percent of all children living at home, and 13 percent of these children live in families where there is no father.[4] In Quebec, where I have my analytical practice, the proportion is higher: one in every six children has no father at home. Twenty percent of all families have just one parent, and 79 percent of these families are headed by women. These families account for 18 percent of the total number of children in Quebec, of whom 14 percent live without their fathers.

In France, according to data based on the 1982 census, 1,307,860 children under the age of 24 live in single-parent families where the parent is a woman. The "Fédération syndicale des familles monoparentales" estimates that in 1988 almost two million children were living with single parents, 85 percent of whom were women. This means that in France some 1,700,000 children were living without fathers. In Switzerland there were 170,485 children living without their fathers in 1980. As astonishing as such figures are, they only take into account situations in which the father is physically absent; they cannot tell us whether the fathers who *are* present in the home are adequate or not.

Absent Fathers

The term *absent fathers* in the title of this book is intended to have a rather broad meaning. It refers to both the psychological and the physical absence of fathers and implies both

---

4. According to the complete data of the 1986 Census, Canada had 4,533,430 families with children: 853,640 were single-parent families, of which 701,905 were headed by women and 151,740 by men. There were 8,578,340 children living in family settings, of whom 1,368,060 were in single-parent families: 1,129,000 in single-parent families headed by women, and 239,065 in single-parent families headed by men. (Source: *Statistics Canada*)

spiritual and emotional absence. It also suggests the notion of fathers who, although physically present, behave in ways that are unacceptable: authoritarian fathers, for example, are oppressive and jealous of their sons' talents and smother their sons' attempts at creativity or self-affirmation. Alcoholic fathers' emotional instability keeps their sons in a permanent state of insecurity.

Lost Sons

The second part of the title, "Lost Sons," is used to underscore the lack of emotional connections between fathers and sons. It is not so much that the sons are lost in any absolute sense, but rather that they have been lost to the fathers they are unconsciously looking for.

This lack of attention from the father results in the son's inability to identify with his father as a means of establishing his own masculine identity. Similarly, a son deprived of the confirmation and security that might have been provided by his father's presence is unable to advance to adulthood. In cases where the father is violent, weak, or continually drunk, the son may find him so repugnant that he will absolutely refuse to identify with the masculine; not only will he hold his father in contempt, but he will also try not to resemble his father in any way whatsoever.

THE FRAGILITY OF MASCULINE IDENTITY

The father's silence dictates the fragility of the son's sexual identity. We know that a personality is constituted and differentiated through a series of identifications. Identification is defined as "a psychological process in which a subject assimilates an aspect, a property, or a characteristic of another and transforms himself totally or partially on the basis of this model."[5] In order to form your own identity, you must identify with someone else; you must structure yourself by incorporating someone else into yourself, by integrating him through imitation.

Before this identification can take place, however, we must have at least vaguely recognized a common element in ourself and the other. This process is impelled by what Freud termed a primal fantasy; through primal fantasy we are connected to the other. This innate tendency, which Jung later called an archetype, enables a son to recognize himself in his father.

Woman Is, Man Is Made

A child's first object relation, his or her first identification, is with the mother. In order to become a "man," however, the young male must proceed from this primary identification with the mother to an identification with the father. This transfer of identification is such a delicate and hazardous process that in tribal societies it is underscored by rites of initiation designed to help the adolescent boy begin his life as an adult man.

The initiation of adolescent males is one of the most highly structured and widespread rituals in the world; rituals for adolescent girls, although they do exist, are not universal and are often less elaborate. Actually, as far as sexual identity is concerned, we might say that women "are," while men have to be "made."[6] The onset of menstruation, which signals the adolescent girl's ability to have children, establishes her feminine identity and provides, as it were, a natural initiation through which she moves from girlhood to womanhood. For men, however, nature has to be supplemented by an educational process in order to transfer the primary identification away from the mother. Initiation rites are intended to mark a

---

5. J. Laplanche and J.-B. Pontalis, *Vocabulaire de la psychanalyse* ("The Vocabulary of Psychoanalysis"), (Paris: Presses Universitaires de France, 1967), p. 184.

6. Anthony Stevens, *Archetypes: A Natural History of the Self*, (New York: William Morrow, 1982), p. 154.

boy's official separation from his mother and his new status as a man.

In actual fact, initiation rites for teenage boys are so widespread that we may well ask ourselves if the masculinity of male children would ever emerge if it weren't forced in this way. Biologists affirm that at the embryonic stage we are all initially female: at the very beginning of pregnancy, the masculine characteristics of an embryo cannot be detected. This seems to suggest that masculinity must be added—and perhaps explains the fragility.

This biological reality seems to explain the fact that masculine identity needs, at least on a psychological level, to be constantly reinforced and regularly supported by other masculine presences in order to remain stable. The existence of some tribes in which the men knit and the women work in the fields suggests that what we know as maleness remains undeveloped unless it is awakened through ritual.

The tribal world sees the identification with the father as subsequent to the identification with the mother. It is also interesting to note that the single-parent family follows the tribal model in that sons, at puberty, often spontaneously express a desire to go to live with their father. In reality, a number of identifications take place simultaneously in the psyche. In order for the son to recognize himself in the father, though, the father has to be present.

The Triangle

In order to evolve, a man has to identify with his mother and with his father. The father-mother-son triangle must replace the mother-son dyad. If the father is absent, however, there is no transfer of identification from the mother to the father, and the son remains imprisoned in his identification with the mother. The father's absence automatically heightens the influence of the mother, who is thus burdened with a responsibility

that will become too heavy for her to bear. In these circumstances the triangle never gets a chance to form properly; the
immediate effect is that, with regard to their sexual identity,
sons develop into giants with feet of clay.

Although mothers have often played leading roles in the
portraits of men in the following pages, it must be kept in
mind that these are three-sided stories: love triangles. Although the literature of psychoanalysis has abundantly described the influence of mothers on their sons, it has in this
regard, often neglected to mention that these mothers were
omnipresent and omnipotent precisely because the fathers
were absent—so absent, in fact, that their absence was simply
taken for granted. These days, when I hear my patients com-
plain about their mothers, what I also hear (although it is not
stated explicitly) is that their fathers were absent. I therefore
ask questions and suggest interpretations aimed at clarifying
the father-child relationship. This is necessary, because the
black hole left by the father's absence is usually filled with
resentment, guilt, idealizations, and mistrust that might otherwise remain unexplored, even in years of therapy. Having a
mother who is dominating, overprotective, repressive, or not
present almost inevitably indicates that the father was absent.

The Present Father

The father is the first significant *other* that the child meets
outside his mother's womb. For the newborn, the father first
of all represents—albeit rather indistinctly—the non-mother;
he incarnates everything that is not her. He becomes the third
character in the love story; he introduces an element of separation between the mother and the child. His very presence
triggers a process of differentiation, since by claiming his wife
he puts an end to the blissful state of symbiosis in which the
mother and child were living: "Your mother is my wife, and
she loves me too!" he says. The child senses that he himself is
no longer the only object of desire. The father, then, embodies
in this way the principles of reality and order in the family.

Second thought suggests, however, that the real separator of the mother and child is not the father, but rather desire—the couple's desire to find each other outside the child.[7] If only as the medium through which this desire is given expression, the father's presence is important. Some fathers put a brutal end to the mother-child symbiosis; this is because they are jealous of the enormous amount of attention showered on the child by their women. As a general rule, however, the couple's amorous desire for each other brings to a halt their exclusive fascination with the child, which the child does need for a certain period of time if he is to get a healthy start in life.

The father helps the child establish an internal structure. More specifically, his presence makes it possible for the child, especially the male child, to develop his own aggressivity (self-affirmation and the capacity for self-defense), his sexuality, his sense of exploration, and his approach to the Logos, or the aptitude for abstraction and objectification.

The father also helps his sons—and his daughters—make the transition from the world of the family to the world of society at large, although the mother too is playing an increasing role in bridging this gap. On the whole, children who have been adequately fathered show more self-confidence, in their studies, in choosing careers, and in their personal initiatives.

A father's love is often expressed in conditional terms, as a way of encouraging the child's achievements: "If you succeed in such and such a thing, I'll give you what you want." The presence of this conditional element is crucial in a child's developing sense of responsibility, a willingness to test and go beyond limits, and even a respect for established hierarchies; however, it will be a positive influence only if it is counterbalanced by affection.

For a father's love to be nonambivalent he has to be properly attentive. He has to spend time with his children—*quality time*

7. I am indebted for this idea to Dr. Elie Humbert, a Jungian analyst in Paris.

is the current catchword. Nine minutes a day for the kids is the length of time American studies have shown is the average father's attentiveness; it is just not enough. The father must show a genuine interest in his children's projects and yet be careful to set certain limits himself. Setting these limits will create the secure atmosphere needed for the child's harmonious development. He must not impose his opinions and decisions by hiding behind his mate; he must reveal his strengths and weaknesses and not be simply evasive, or worse, stubbornly authoritarian.

By being open about his own imperfections the father reveals to his child a real world in which he (the child) is not always expected to be perfect. It shows the child that the exercise of power does not have to be humiliating, that healthy competition and emulation do not always lead to stomach ulcers, and that ability can be a source of joy, not of alienation. "Acts of fatherhood are acts that balance support and care against the need to set limits for childish dependency."[8]

Inadequate Fathering

An inadequate father is one who behaves in unacceptable ways toward his son. Following is a summary of the ways in which fathers can impose great frustration on their children.

1. The prolonged absence of the father for whatever reason. The child may be simply abandoned, or he may be confined to a hospital or institution for a long period.

2. The father's unresponsiveness to the child's need for affection and attachment. The father is unresponsive to the child's care-eliciting behavior and may actively reject him.

3. The father's threats of abandonment, which are used to coerce or discipline the child. These may take the form of threats to abandon the family, to withdraw his love, to commit suicide if his child continues to act in a certain way, or even to kill his mate or his child.

---

8. Stephen A. Shapiro, *Manhood, a New Definition* (New York: G. P. Putnam's Sons, 1984), p. 97.

4. The father's induction of guilt in the child. Assertions are made that the child's behavior is or will be responsible for the illness or death of one of the parents.

5. The father clinging on to the child. In the case of an alcoholic father, for instance, the child may be forced into a parental role, and must grow up too quickly.

These attitudes or actions, categorized by Anthony Stevens,[9] provide an eloquent summary of the principal traumas described by patients in therapy. I would add two others to the list: fathers who regularly beat their sons, and fathers who make them into scapegoats for everything that is wrong in the family.

Behavior of this sort from the father causes the son to lack self-confidencce, to be excessively timid, and to have difficulties in adapting to new circumstances. The son will often remain immature and overly dependent, given to anxieties, depression, obsessions, compulsions, and phobias. In addition, he will tend to repress his rage strongly. His deep need for love may also take bizarre forms such as halfhearted attempts at suicide, running away from home, feigned illnesses, wild accusations, and all sorts of manipulations.

We should also note that, to the extent these disorders are caused by the father's "absence," they will be compensated to the same extent by an unconscious process of idealization. A boy whose father has left home will tend either to idealize the father or to seek an ideal father-substitute. Often he will be so blinded by his desire that he will be unable to assess accurately the father figures he has chosen, and this will lead to yet another betrayal by the substitute father.

What the Research Shows

Sons who have not been given adequate fathering are often faced with the following problems: in their teenage years they

---

9. Stevens, *Archetypes,* p. 111. I have adapted these elements to father-son relationships, but they also apply equally well to the relationships between mothers and their children.

experience confusion about their sexual identity and adopt feminine types of behavior; their sense of self-esteem is unsteady; they repress their aggressivity (and, consequently, their need for self-affirmation), their ambition, and their inquisitiveness. Some of them may suffer from inhibitions with regard to their sexuality. They may also exhibit learning problems. They have trouble respecting moral values and accepting responsibilities; they have little sense of duty or obligation toward others. The absence of limits also makes it difficult for them to act with authority or to respect the authority of others. Their insufficient internal structure results in a certain laxity, a lack of rigor, a general inability to organize their lives effectively. In addition, research has shown they are more likely to be homosexuals than are boys whose fathers are sufficiently present. Inadequately fathered sons are also more apt to develop psychological problems,[10] that manifest as juvenile delinquency and abuse of drugs and alcohol. All such behaviors are rooted in deep revolt against patriarchal society. This revolt mirrors to the father the consequences of his absence.

Starting Out with Daddy

Until fairly recently, psychologists believed that the role of the father in a child's life began when the child was three or four and able to speak. Some psychoanalysts actually considered a father's part-time presence in the family to be a beneficial and necessary frustration for the child. In the past thirty years, however, research into the psychology of child development has come up with some surprising new information.

In the United States and Norway, several studies involving boys with behavioral problems arrived at conclusions that flew in the face of accepted belief: male children absolutely need

---

10. Henry B. Biller, "Fatherhood: Implications for Child and Adult Development," *Handbook of Developmental Psychology*, ed. Benjamin B. Wolman (Englewood Cliffs, N.J.: Prentice-Hall, 1982), pp. 711–714.

their fathers in the first two years of their existence. The boys in the studies all experienced absent fathers in the first two years of their lives. In most cases their fathers were soldiers who had gone away when their sons were still very young, or sailors who were away from home nine months a year. What is striking is that these boys showed the same kinds of atypical development as orphans in inadequate foster homes or as boys brought up in single-parent families and deprived of possible father-substitutes. In all sons who lack fathers, research has revealed systematic deficiencies on social, sexual, moral, or cognitive levels.

Henry Biller, who has conducted several of these studies, makes the following observation: "Boys who experienced father-absence before the age of two were more handicapped in terms of several dimensions of personality development than were boys who experienced father-absence at a later age. For example, boys who experienced father-absence before age two were found to be less trusting, less industrious, and to have more feelings of inferiority than boys who experienced father-absence between the ages of three and five."[11]

The same author stresses the fact that numerous studies have shown that a warm, affectionate relationship between a father and son results in a stronger development of the son's masculine identity. He adds that the sense of limits and discipline imposed by the father will only be effective in the context of a loving relationship; in other contexts this sense may actually prevent the son from imitating his father.

Biller considers the quality of the father-son relation to be just as important to the son's development as the father's very presence. Though a father may have proved his independence and competence in the workplace, if he comes home from work, simply plunks himself in front of the TV and does not participate actively in the family, his son may well turn out to be passive and withdrawn.

---

11. Ibid., p. 706.

It is interesting to note, however, that sons whose fathers have died are exceptions to the general rule. In spite of the complete absence of their fathers they show fewer difficulties in adaptation than sons whose fathers are absent for other reasons. It seems that widows often have very positive memories of their husbands, and that they talk a lot about them; for their sons this helps create a positive symbolic image of the father that partially compensates for the fact that he is not present.

Indirectly, this research shows how necessary it is for parents who have split up to settle their differences, or at the very least to avoid denigrating the absent parent in front of the children. For sons and daughters, the way the mother talks about the absent father and the respect she may or may not have for him are crucial in their forming a positive image of the masculine. The reverse is also true, of course.

It is also absolutely essential for a single parent to explain objectively to the children why the other parent is absent or rarely present. This explanation helps reduce the feelings of guilt or diminished self-worth children may experience as a result of their parents' failings. Children often interpret these feelings as results of their own bad behavior; children may simply feel not important or good enough to deserve their parents' care and attention. It is always the children who end up paying for the problems parents don't want to talk about.

THE FATHER'S BODY

One of the major consequences of a father's absence is that his sons are deprived of their bodies. Because the body is the foundation of all identity, identity must begin to take shape with the body. The identity of the son is rooted in the body of the father.

Men's Bodies Belong to Their Mothers

Since the mother creates the child in her body, the areas of the body he associates with her are internal ones. The areas he associates with the father are external ones. The mother, of course, enjoys a special closeness with the child when he is still in her womb, and she prolongs this relationship after the child is born. She changes the baby's diapers, cuddles him, rocks him to sleep, and sings to him. In short, with her direct access to his body, she imbues him with herself in every possible way.

The father, on the other hand, often remains outside. His sperm enters the woman from the outside, and immediately after the birth he is again pushed aside: his mate clings to the baby as her own personal possession. The plan, though, had been to have the baby together as a couple. The father's remaining outside may not disturb him: another mouth to feed may mean he has to work a little harder than before, in which case he may accept the situation. If he does not, he may find himself a frustrated, "thwarted father"[12] who is kept away from his child's body by the possessiveness of his mate. In any case, as long as the child remains in the family setting, the situation will probably remain basically the same: the child will have a lot of contact with his mother and very little with his father.

The major result of this is that *the son will not develop positively in relation to his father's body, but rather will develop negatively against his mother's body and against the female body in general*. At this point the love story between the mother and the son turns into a power struggle, and the son begins his war against women. The ridiculous thing about this war is that it stems from a complete misunderstanding: the realm of the body, of the senses and feelings, is thought to belong exclusively to women, and the realm of the mind, of the external world and the workplace, is relegated exclusively to men. Sensuality and sensitivity are a human heritage that certainly doesn't belong exclusively to men or to women.

At an even deeper level this causes disruptions in the way

12. The expression is borrowed from Olivier, "Thwarted Fathers," pp. 201–207.

men view their own bodies and results in *a repression of all sensuality and all "corporality."* In the son's mind, men cannot allow themselves to touch, caress, smell, feel, laugh, or cry, because these are things he has seen only his mother do. The adolescent boy will try to deny he has a body. He will even attempt to repress his strong, nascent sexual drive, which is considered sinful. Later in his life, when he makes love, he will concentrate on genital pleasure and be careful not to let his excitement or playfulness go too far beyond the erogenous zones, for fear of acting too much like a woman. Only when he is completely alone will he allow himself a sensuality he considers shameful. Otherwise he will take up forms of pleasure that permit men to be sensual without their being perceived as sissies: appreciation of good food and fine wines, for example.

The first result of fathers' leaving their sons to the exclusive care of their mothers is the sons' fear of women, and particularly their fear of being women. The second result is that, all through their lives, the sons will have a fear of bodies—women's bodies and their own.

The Father's Heart

The son who is frightened of his body will be even more frightened of his heart. We have to keep in mind that, in our culture, being a man means "not expressing emotion." Masculinity is thus defined in negative terms: it is not to cry, not to listen to yourself, not to speak of your feelings, not to look too feminine. Real men don't eat quiche. Real men don't dance. In other words, our masculine identity is based on blocking any expression of our bodies and emotions. This rigidity and imperviousness form the foundations upon which men build their identity. It is not that men have no sensitivity; it is rather that they are forbidden to express it if they want to be considered men by other men. In this sense, becoming a man requires cutting oneself off succcessfully from both heart and body. In fact one is all the more a man if he manages this amputation without crying or complaining.

Ironically, men are then expected to have a capacity for intimacy with their partners and their children. How in the world can a person who has cut himself off from his body and heart—and been admired for this by society—aspire to intimacy with anybody?

As long as fathers do not incorporate the other side of the masculine, the side that is capable of love and tenderness, there will be no significant change in the male community—or in relationships between men and women. Fathers becoming emotionally present for their sons and daughters seems to me one of the few possible solutions to the growing problems of interpersonal relations in our society.

Men are cut off from their emotions because they have not seen their fathers or other men expressing inner feelings. Fortunately, with the breakdown of patriarchal values that has resulted in large part from the feminist movement, more and more men are aware of their being emotional cripples. More and more of them are refusing to stifle their sensitivity.

Fear of Homosexuality

What happens to those parts of ourselves we have amputated or chosen to ignore? They form what Jung calls our shadow; in order to free ourselves of this uncomfortable shadow, we project it outside ourselves onto people of the same sex. We see in them the parts of ourselves we don't like, conveniently forgetting that these parts exist within us. Having been conditioned to repress their emotional and erotic nature, men often aggressively project the unaccepted dimensions of their personalities onto homosexuals.

These projections (like actual projectiles) are apparent in the fear and fascination homosexuality exerts on men in general. The more a heterosexual denies his body and his heart, the more likely he is to hate homosexuals and use them as scapegoats. Homophobia and the fact that society often considers homosexuality to be a pathological condition simply reveal men's fear of their repressed emotions and desires.

This projection of the shadow is also undifferentiated; the whole shadow gets projected, including its most repugnant elements. For example: many governmental and volunteer organizations responsible for finding substitute fathers for needy boys refuse to consider openly homosexual men for these roles. The unacknowledged prejudice inherent in such policies is that homosexuals are perverts, incapable of controlling themselves sexually. This prejudice remains unshaken, in spite of the statistics showing that the vast majority of child molestation cases are committed by timid, frustrated heterosexuals. This prejudice shows how powerful and totally irrational our projections can be. Men in our society often expect the worst of homosexuals; they are ready to blame them for everything under the sun. This is revolting.

As a consequence of this situation, a lack of physical affection from the father gives rise to another fear in the son, although here the right word is not fear, but terror: the terror of being homosexual. Every human being, in fact, feels an erotic impulse toward others of the same sex. This impulse accounts for the feelings of affection, friendship, and admiration we have for people of our own sex. We are afraid of recognizing this aspect of ourselves, however; we prefer instead to project it on to homosexuals. We make the mistake of confusing masculine identity with sexual orientation. A man's homosexuality does not make him any less a man or any less a decent human being, but our culture still blindly refuses to recognize this.

The fear of being homosexual is so deeply entrenched in men, so insidious and persistent, that it ends up haunting all the friendly bonds men have with other men. It poisons all possibility of masculine eroticism, and it prevents many fathers from touching their sons.

Men are thus caught in a classic double bind. As soon as a man approaches the realm of his sensitivity, he finds himself confronted by his latent homosexuality, which is all the more powerful because all his potential sensuality has been relegated to it. In extreme terms, a man who wants to repossess his physical senses has no choice but to become a homosexual or to risk being taken for one by other men and sometimes even by women.

The French psychoanalyst Annette Fréjaville believes that in the very first months of his life, the formation of a boy's sexual identity requires mutual idealizations between father and son. She calls this "primary homosexuality": "My son's going to be an engineer when he grows up!" "I want to be just like daddy when I grow up!" She also speaks of the necessity of a "love story" involving the father and son at the time when the son is just beginning to speak. This love story will promote genital development at a time when sexual differentiation has barely begun to take place. This "primary homosexuality" will later provide the son with greater assurance in his life as a heterosexual, should he be a heterosexual.

A study of teenage homosexual boys at the college level revealed that most of them were highly gifted and hypersensitive. This seems to me an essential point: these boys turned to homosexual behavior because they were unable to find their own sensitivity reflected in their fathers. Since men have been conditioned to repress any open expression of their sensitivity, their sons cannot identify with them: their sons do not find the similarity which is the basis of all identification. These highly gifted youngsters fail to recognize themselves in the traditional roles assigned to men, and consequently they reject participating in social institutions such as marriage and the family.

I tend to believe that homosexuality in men expresses the need for a firm grounding in the masculine, in that which is similar to one's own self. Homosexuality may thus be said to express an unconscious search for the father and for a male identity.

Homosexuals are not different than heterosexual men; like

heterosexuals, they are sons who are still trying to wrest their bodies away from the clutches of their mothers, or they are men who are fed up with having to live according to the dictates of a society that denies them access to their physical senses. Homosexuals are denigrated by a society that cannot figure out how it came to produce so many of them, yet they may well be at the forefront of men's struggle to take possession of their own bodies and their own hearts.

Polluting the Body of the Earth

The denial of the body also has disastrous consequences at the collective level, at which men's desperate attempts to avoid assimilation by their mothers' bodies is reflected, in part, by their contempt for the body of Mother Earth. Could it be that the pillage and pollution of the earth by gray-suited men at the helm of huge corporations express the unconscious revenge of sons against the female body? Does this lack of respect, this abuse of power by the human animal toward his own habitat, stem from the crazy position at which men have arrived through their depriving themselves of the sensations of their bodies? Is it their cries of rage that pierce holes in the ozone layer? Have men been driven to such brutal destructiveness by the tremendous pain of being cut off from their own sensitivity, by the denial of their sensitivity by their unsuspecting parents? Is this kind of behavior not typical of children or animals who have been deprived of affection all their lives?

In Praise of Modern Fathers

It is commonly claimed that "mothering fathers" cannot provide a solution to that problem. But men who have decided to share equal responsibility with the mother for the physical care of a child are not simply imitating the maternal model. I believe this to be an error in judgment. If this is not the solution to the problem of disincarnated sons, then what *is*? Again, are we not victims of the old bias that assigns to women the "internal" and to men the "external"? A father who takes care of his child physically and emotionally is not a mothering father, but a *father* pure and simple—he gives reality to a word that until now has remained practically empty of meaning.

"Each parent serves a double function: as a bodily reference point for a child of the same sex, and as the locus of desire for a child of the opposite sex."[13] This bodily reference point in the parent of the same sex acts as a foundation for sexual identity. If well grounded, this foundation will in turn allow the child to feel desire for the parent of the opposite sex. A son who is familiar with the physical presence of his father is thus initially able to love his mother and later in life to desire women rather than fearing or despising them.

I spoke earlier of the difficulties involved in shifting the son's identification from the mother to the father. This transfer is clearly less precarious and more likely to occur naturally if the father is physically present with his son from the very beginning. The pitched battles that often take place between teenage boys and their mothers are signs that the sons are trying in every possible way to escape from maternal domination, trying to wrest their bodies away from their mothers, and trying to prove themselves as men. The fathers usually feel powerless to do anything but watch these hostilities from the sidelines, unaware that they themselves are largely responsible for those hostilities. These situations often indicate that the sons are repressing their gentler emotions and imitating the worst macho stereotypes our society has produced—like Rambo and his cohorts—just to prove they are "man enough."

It seems obvious that a father doesn't take care of a child in exactly the same way as a mother does. Even if he does, though, what counts for the son is to be exposed to the father's smell, to hear his deeper voice, and to tumble about in his arms—fathers are more likely than mothers to play with their children physically. The father who cuddles his child is obviously in no danger of losing the things that make him

---

13. Olivier, "Thwarted Fathers." p. 206.

different from his child: the hairiness of his body, his ability to produce sperm, his hormonal system—the undeniable marks of his masculinity.

It is absolutely necessary for men to spend more time cuddling their children, especially their sons; doing so they will open up their children's sensitivity—and discover their own sensitivity at the same time. Sensuality will then no longer be denied to men and women will no longer be trapped in it. Men too have bodies; they need to be touched in order to maintain their sense of well-being and in order to be reminded that they are alive.

Men are frightened of becoming fathers because they don't want their sons to have to go through the same torments that they themselves experienced—their being forced to shoulder endless responsibilities and to remain cut off from their feelings. At the same time men are aware of the cost of overcoming their fears and of raising children who will be in touch with their own sensitivity. Men sense their old terror coming back—the terror of *being* women. They will have to confront this terror if they decide to reclaim their rightful place by their children. Modern fathers and concerned couples have to fight hard to change their own attitudes: this is one of our only hopes for survival.

THE MISSING STRUCTURE

The father's silence, whether verbal or physical, also has repercussions on the inner world of his son—especially the structuring of his son's psyche. Let's see how this works.

Archetypes

Like animals, human beings have certain predetermined patterns of behavior that will be activated at appropriate moments. These patterns are common to the entire human race and represent life's basic programs. Triggered by experiences resulting from contacts with the external environment, these forms of behavior are called instincts.

In the same way that instincts govern our behavior, there are also innate patterns that govern our ways of feeling and thinking. Jung called these "archetypes." The tendency for the psyche to pre-form its contents shows itself in images or ideas. For example: the human mind usually functions by comparing opposites such as hot and cold or high and low; similarly, humans generally react in the universal ways to love, danger, or death, without anyone having had to teach them these ways of reacting.

Archetypes, which like all behavior patterns are impersonal and collective, need to be personalized, or experienced through a relation. A good example of this phenomenon is the love relation, with the whole gamut of fantasies, emotions, and idealizations that necessarily accompany it.

The newborn infant is preconditioned to meet a father and mother in his environment, since he carries these archetypes within him. To actualize his potential, he has to meet someone in his surroundings whose behavior is sufficiently like that of a father or mother to "turn on the program." The result of this meeting between the inborn basic structure and the actual parents is what we call a father complex or a mother complex.

Satan or Superman

As I explored the theme of masculine identity with a group of men, it became apparent to me that each one of us was grappling with a model of masculinity that he could not live up to. This model consisted of an ideal image that oppressed us from within—an unconscious image that we tried to respond to without being aware of doing so.

What lies behind these unconscious models? The need for a father is a basic human archetypal need. When this need is not personalized by a father's presence, it remains a crude need, nourished only by cultural images of the father ranging from the Devil to the Heavenly Father. The more the father is absent, the less chance the child will have of humanizing him, and the more the unconscious need will express itself in primitive images. These images will exert a great amount of pressure on the child's unconscious. They will take the forms of mythic characters such as Superman, Rambo, and the Incredible Hulk.

When an archetype has not been humanized it remains divided into a pair of opposites; these are extremely potent forces that tyrannize the ego and wrench it in opposite directions. The father's presence, though, allows the child to unite these opposing elements that condition the child's psyche. It is the father's humanity that enables the son to conceive of a world in which things are not all black and white, and in which opposites can be juxtaposed and reconciled.

This unconscious model is probably at the source of the inner voice that constantly tells a male that he is not really a man. In real terms, the unfulfilled archetype and the images it produces condemn a man to being an "eternal son" or "substandard" male—until the man becomes conscious of what is happening to him. The son has doubts about his own virility. He remains distant from others and unpredictable, since his only male model has been a disincarnated image of the father, and not a father in flesh and blood.

The Incest Taboo

As Freud stressed in his study of the Oedipus complex in boys, the father's presence blocks access to the symbiotic satisfaction the child naturally seeks, and in doing so, it inseparably links desire and the law. For the child, the father represents an initial prohibition: the incest taboo.

This taboo is decisive at the psychological level because it structures the boy's psychological universe. By putting an end to the complete fusion between the mother and her child, the father thus quashes the identification between desire and the object of desire. This means that the child can become aware of desire as a *psychological fact* that exists on its own, independent of the desire's finding satisfaction or not in external reality. This frustration creates, as it were, an internal space, that gives birth to the son's inner world. The fusion between the ego[15] and the unconscious[16] is thus broken; this break is of capital importance in structuring the psyche.

When a man remains identified with his mother, he remains fused with his unconscious: he *is* his own desires, his own impulses, his own ideas. He has no sense of them as internal objects that do not necessarily have to be obeyed.

The frustration of the child's incestuous desire also allows nature to be separated from culture. A man who lives in symbiosis with his inner world is also in symbiosis with the outer world. He becomes his culture and finds himself identified with its prevailing stereotypes: if being a man means being macho, he will be macho; if it means being gentle, he will be gentle. In other words, a man who is principally identified with his mother has no access to his own individuality. He remains subject to his unconscious and to the whims of social fashion. In technical terms, he will be dominated internally by

---

15. The ego is the center of the field of consciousness. It is itself a complex, based on the experience of a sense of individual identity and of continuation in time; it is what enables a person to recognize himself in the mirror day after day and to make the connection between the child he was and the adult he has become. The ego seeks to maintain what might be thought of as an even temperature (homeostasis); it possesses defense mechanisms to regulate its equilibrium. However, it may happen that these mechanisms become too rigid and suffocate the ego instead of protecting it.

16. *Unconscious* is a technical term that simply means everything outside of consciousness. It is impossible to wipe it clean since, by analogy, consciousness is like a little island floating on the surface of the sea of the unconscious. The unconscious contains everything that was previously conscious and is now forgotten, as well as all the experiences that were repressed because the ego found them unpleasant. It also includes a collective layer containing the structural preconditionings of the human psyche (collective complexes, i.e., archetypes). Jung considers the unconscious to be basically creative in that it produces new ideas and intuitions that have never been conscious. The self is the center for the entire personality. Therapy aims at establishing a relationship between the ego and the self.

a mother complex. Since the mother is virtually the only reference point for such a son, she will also loom large in his psyche. The son's ego thus runs the risk of remaining a little boy in relation to the overly powerful mother complex.

Complexes

Complexes provide the structure for our psychological organism—they are the backbone of our inner reality. They are negative only when they cause us to behave in ways that are problematic. Complexes are always centered on an emotional experience that was strong enough to have formed a magnet-like core that will attract all experiences of the same emotional color. Of course, the child's relations with both his mother and his father fall into the category of primordial experiences and will thus automatically lead to the formation of complexes.

A complex is an internalization[17] of the relation we have had with someone. Complexes do not tell us what the father and the mother actually were, but rather what the relation with them was. This relation is made up of many elements unconnected with the parents' personalities; an accident that leaves the child in the hospital for several weeks, for instance, or a mother's nervous breakdown or the death of a father. Take the example of Andy:

Andy, who was forty years old, often felt an uncontrollable fear of being abandoned, for no apparent reason. He was literally afraid of disappearing. He also had severe doubts about his sensory perceptions. The problem did not seem to stem from his parental environment. However, when he was six months old his parents had been forced to flee their country

---

17. I use the word *internalize* in the sense of introjection. Introjection is operating, for example, when the external mother who may have been overly demanding of her child becomes an internal character who continues to demand things of him even though he is no longer a child and is no longer living near his mother. The mother thus becomes a component of the psyche; she becomes a complex—an alter ego or secondary character operating within the individual.

because of war and had placed him in a foster home. There he found himself in the presence of an old couple who quarrelled incessantly. Thus, just as he had begun to form an identity through eye contact and interaction with his parents, his world suddenly, completely disappeared.

We can hardly blame Andy's parents, who had done what they could to ensure their child's survival under the circumstances. Nevertheless, an experience of this kind has a negative impact on the child at the psychological level. The feeling of being abandoned at an early age actually provided the core for negative parental complexes that colored this patient's entire emotional life and taught him an absolute mistrust of all forms of emotional attachment. His fear of disappearing was a symbolic expression of what had happened to him.

Strictly speaking, complexes are not carbon copies of relationships with the father and the mother, since other people also influence complexes. A father complex is actually the sum total of everything that a child has experienced in relation to the paternal order, including, for instance, a grandfather, a teacher, or an older brother. A mother complex is similar in its composition.

It is extremely important to understand the difference between a real parent and a parental complex, because once we reach a certain point, our vision of reality is influenced not by our objective parents but rather by our complexes. These complexes fix us on certain wavelengths. For example, a man who has been subjected to his father's brutality sees only the brute in his father and the brutality of men in general. He only notices the negative sides of his father; as the years go by, the conviction that men can only be brutal strengthens his complex.

Our inner life is governed by the alter egos that constitute our complexes; the solution to this situation is to become sufficiently conscious of the complexes so that the ego has room to breathe in its own house. By accepting its relation with its internal partners, the ego avoids their forcing him to feel and to see one-sidedly. If these complexes remain autonomous, however, they take over and force us to repeat the same patterns endlessly.

A Healthy Personality

A healthy ego is one that remains flexible. In fact, psychological flexibility is what defines mental health. The ego may be alternately strong or vulnerable; it may voluntarily open up to receive what is rising from the depths, and it may choose to accept what rises up, oppose it, or to negotiate some intermediate position with it. Jung insisted repeatedly on this point: the process of integrating the energy of complexes is a process of confrontation with the unconscious. Actually, confrontation may be too strong a word. The term used by Jung, *Auseinandersetzung,* implies the image of two people who sit down face to face in order to get to the bottom of a question, to explain what they mean, and to reach a new way of looking at things.

Since neither the ego nor the internal partner sees things completely accurately, some combination of the two must be reached. It is important to avoid adopting a viewpoint that is excessively favorable to the unconscious—this leads the individual into the realms of prophecy and magic—or a viewpoint that is excessively unfavorable—this leads the individual to exaggerate rationality to the point where he is completely dried up as a person.

We have to develop a relationship with our inner self. In my opinion, this relationship is the area in which Jung made his most important contribution to depth psychology; for Jung it was impossible to try to control the unconscious; rather he stressed the establishment of a living relationship with it. This suggests the idea of psychological ecology.

After three years of therapy, Bert, a fifty-five-year-old, has managed to work out an acceptable attitude toward himself. Previously he had a virulent, obsessive self-hatred. He blamed and criticized himself in a thousand ways every time anything went wrong. Each failure was like a ton of bricks falling on his head. His self-hatred destabilized him to the point that he would actually forget what it had been that set off each sudden, self-destructive crisis. "Today," he says, "I understand myself better. When I hate myself, I talk to myself gently, and slowly move away from whatever was weighing me down." His ego has managed to find a comfortable position with respect to his unconscious, and to remain flexible against its attacks. Bert no longer lets himself get crushed by the ton of bricks: now he can relate to his inner world.

Lacking a Father Is Like Lacking a Backbone

An individual's psychological identity is based on his sense of his own spine, that provides him with support from the inside. The father's absence results in the child's lack of internal structure; this is the very essence of a negative father complex. An individual with a negative father complex does not feel himself structured from within. His ideas are confused; he has trouble setting himself goals, making choices, deciding what is good for him, and identifying his own needs. For him, everything gets mixed up: love and reason, sexual appetites and the simple need for affection. He sometimes has problems concentrating, he is distracted by all sorts of insignificant details, and in severe cases he has difficulty organizing his perceptions. Basically he never feels sure about anything.

The distinguishing feature of this negative father complex is an internal disorder that can range from a slight sense of confusion to serious mental disorganization. Men who are faced with a negative father complex will attempt to compensate for it by structuring themselves from the outside. This external structuring, however, will take on different accents, depending on whether the individual is a Mr. Nice Guy, an obnoxious drunk, or some other type.

Take, for example, the hero types who always have some important task to accomplish and who scramble around like industrious ants, making sure they never have an empty moment. They find their support in the admiration of others, which is why they pay so much attention to society's values. Don Juan types, on the other hand, structure themselves with their frequent sexual exploits. They live for sexual thrills and fill up their days—and their lives—chasing after them. This pursuit becomes a major physical and mental occupation, and acts as a structuring element. Other men structure themselves with physical exercise like bodybuilding, which serves to compensate for internal weakness by building up the outside of the body.

The more fragile a man feels internally, the more likely he is to try building an outer shell to hide this fragility. This shell may take the form of bulging muscles or a bulging belly. Similarly, the more categorical, direct, and outspoken a man's opinions are, the more they mask a basic lack of certainty. Rebellious sons try to structure themselves by joining gangs that are essentially fascist; they give obedience to a primitive father. Eternal adolescents, they are really looking for spiritual masters despite their apparent anarchy. Alcoholics' inner turmoil is usually all too obvious.

By means of these outward compensations, lost sons attempt to ignore their craving for love and understanding, their deep desire to be touched, their need to love and be loved. It is hard for them to face up to these feelings because this facing-up makes them feel vulnerable. The signature of a missing father is the fragile masculine identity of his sons.

TWO

Lost Sons

THE THEATER OF VIRILITY

A Word of Welcome

Ladies and gentlemen, welcome to the Theater of Virility! Tonight the Dads and Lads Company is presenting *Lost Sons,* a group production based on improvisations by the actors.

The play shows ten men of today who are having problems dealing with themselves. The portraits are timeless ones: they depict common manifestations of maleness that have remained unchanged over the centuries. As we see these men acting out their lives—all the world's a stage, as Shakespeare said—we also see different facets of ourselves acting on our own inner stages. In fact the play is a kind of game in which we can gauge how much we identify with the various characters. So just sit back and choose your own blend of male stereotypes.

A Word from the Director

While working with this company I found myself in a situation that was so comical and yet so alarming that I didn't know whether to laugh or cry. The moment I set foot in the theater, I realized the actors seemed to be endlessly rehearsing scenes from plays they had been repeating ever since their childhood. There was nothing I could do to prevent this. Since they appeared determined to act out their pasts, and since we couldn't agree on a form for the show, I decided to make a virtue of necessity and concentrate on shaping the material that emerged from their improvisations.

Such peculiar circumstances necessitate these few words of somewhat analytic explanation. To begin with, all the actors had fathers who were more or less absent; this explains why they now often have excessive reactions to father figures. Some of the characters respond to figures of authority with hate or admiration; they are insulting them or totally subservient to these figures. Other characters display a cold indifference which never completely hides the emotions boiling inside them. They all suffer from a serious lack of self-esteem.

It would seem, in fact, that sons who had inadequate relationships with their fathers have actually been left with psychological holes that quickly fill up with dangerous fantasies about masculinity. This much I can assure you from my own experience: never in my life have I had so much trouble gaining the respect of a bunch of actors! Some of them got absolutely paranoid about me, others acted as though I were some kind of magician. Most of the actors didn't trust the other actors they were working with!

Another peculiarity is that each of my actors was struggling with an invisible character who forced him to go on repeating the same script constantly. Take Bob, for example. He told me about how, when his mother was suffering from a terrible depression, he started memorizing little skits as a way of earning her affection and making her laugh; after a while, of course, the little skits became big skits—that's always the way with actors—and his behavior became more and more like that of a hero. Unfortunately, there was no one around to tell him he could stop acting; no one told him he was fine just the way he was, and that he didn't need to put on a show to attract attention. So now Bob just keeps on playing the role of a hero.

Out of desperation I invited one of my psychoanalyst friends to a rehearsal, hoping he could help me understand what was going on. This friend told me that each actor was possessed by a complex. He used the word "possessed" about Bob, for example, in this sense: Bob isn't aware that he is constantly repeating the same role. Bob didn't choose to play the hero; rather it is as though the hero script chose him and has kept him imprisoned in itself.

By observing Bob, I came to understand that a complex is a mechanical pattern of reaction that is automatically triggered for an individual as soon as he finds himself in a situation similar to one he has encountered in the past. Whenever Bob is in a situation even remotely reminiscent of one he has experienced with his mother, he starts behaving blindly, as if he has taken leave of his senses. Not realizing that it's a new situation, he acts as if he were still in the old one. Sometimes he actually *chooses* situations and partners that remind him of his past. For example, in one of the improvisations he decided to work heroically for a company that constantly needed to be saved from bankruptcy; as if that weren't enough, he also chose to live with a woman who was having severe psychological problems. Bob could no longer distinguish between himself and the character he was playing.

The psychoanalyst concluded, "It would be a good idea for you to remind the audience that each of the actors is at least partly responsible for the script that has made him a victim. After all, the troubles he had with his parents often come from his refusal to face up to the problems in his own personality."

"That's a bit heavy, isn't it?" I replied. "You keep talking about problems, problems, and more problems, but in fact these people *need* to play these roles in their lives. If they weren't playing heroes or seducers—if they weren't drunk or suicidal—they would be overcome with anxiety and feel as though they had no structure or foundation. It seems to me that their suffering doesn't come from the kinds of roles they have to play: after all, we all have to play some kind of role in life. I think their suffering does not come from the characters that haunt them either, nor does it come from their unwillingness to accept their own share of responsibility. No, their suffering is caused by close identification with roles from their pasts—extreme levels of identification keep them repeating the same scenarios over and over again."

"So how do *you* explain this identification?" he asked. "It certainly seems rather . . . complex!"

Synopsis of the Play

The inadequate father is distinguished by his physical or mental absence, his tyranny or alcoholism, his defeatist or spineless personality. He has probably not been able to act as a natural trigger for his son for the genetic and psychological program we might call "how to become a man." The model he provided has turned out to be deficient, and consequently he has not initiated his son. The son, therefore, has identified largely with the feminine and has repressed his own masculinity. He has taken refuge in an eternal adolescence and has tended to reject traditionally masculine values. He has thus remained cut off from his own sense of self-affirmation and exploration.

Now let's see what our actors are up to. We find them acting out their lives as adults, unable to shake themselves free of the ghosts that haunt their existence. Remember, when they go on and on talking about their mothers, they are really talking about their missing fathers.

BOB THE HERO

Bob comes from a race of heroes. How handsome they are, how strong and proud! They arrive all decked out with their weapons and armor. Some come equipped with gleaming new BMWs, others are armed with sharp minds and scathing wit, and still others have developed amazing bodies with tremendous physical strength. All of them are engaged in an endless battle.

The fields of battle are different for the different heroes, however. Some head dynamic young companies; they are out to make money and gain reputation. Others are committed to idealistic causes; they are ready to lay down their lives for their beliefs. They work for Amnesty International or for the independence of their homelands. Some of the more modest ones limit their bravery to talking more than anyone else at a party or drinking a maximum amount of beer in a minimum amount of time.

They often feel responsible for their fellow man. They like to lead things: political gatherings, business meetings, or evenings with friends. Their zeal often greatly benefits mankind, and some of them end up widely revered. Others remain the eternal life-of-the-party, hearty, jovial . . . and obnoxious.

Heroes possess strength, determination, and courage. They are the sons of Hera, Queen of Olympus, from whom they take their name. Hera is the mother who inspires them, and in fact the hero is always trying to live up to the heroic wishes of his mother. She's the one who pumps him full of ambition and courage. Just think of Rose Kennedy or Lillian Carter, women who supported their sons through thick and thin, and who in a sense sacrificed them to the nation.

The mother of a hero is often a demanding person who has had great ambitions for her son ever since his early childhood. It is sometimes said that this type of woman is possessed by her animus, her masculine side, and that she transmits to her son the dreams she had for herself. Mothers of heroes are not generally affectionate or accommodating as mothers; in fact they're more likely to be tough, no-nonsense types, who are so proud of their offspring that they try to make them into divine beings. The young hero thus finds himself trapped, in his heart of hearts, by the desire to please his mother, to fulfill her ambitions. He tries to satisfy the ambitions of his real mother, then, very soon he starts aiming to satisfy the highest demands of his society, business, social group, or university.

Bob the Hero always wants to be on top of things, and in this way he often becomes a real source of inspiration for his admirers. As a child he lived for the approval of his mother; now he lives for the approval of others. This is what keeps him going. So that everyone will love and appreciate him, he performs the most difficult exploits. Admirable in himself, he feeds on the admiration of others. In a symbolic sense, he wants to personify the strong, erect penis that will be the envy of other men!

Deep within himself, however, the hero sometimes suffers from a terrible feeling of guilt about his father; he feels that he has betrayed his father by responding to the idealized projections of his mother. Having supplanted his father in the eyes of his mother, he fears reprisals. If he has the choice, he surrounds himself with women; his relations with men remain troubled and ambiguous. Often he tries to make amends by suffering a terrible defeat that will lead to his being judged by paternal-type authorities.

The Drama of the Public Person

Bob is an actor with a brilliant international career. His childhood was particularly difficult, since he had to be supportive of a mother who was both depressive and demanding. He also had to face rejection from his father, who found him effeminate. Bob told me about a dream he had when he was offered the directorship of a college theater department: he had just been elected president; from now on he would have to assume a great many responsibilities and put aside his sex life. The evening before he dreamed this dream he had consciously thought about needing to break up with his girlfriend, since she was a student in the same school at which he would be working.

When Bob is exposed to public opinion, his image problem becomes quite severe: he feels obliged to rein in his aggressivity and sexuality. He thus manages to respond to the requirements of society, but in doing so he loses his individuality. He rises to the top of the heap, but at the same time he spoils his enjoyment of life.

Solitude, paradoxically, is often the ambiguous reward for the life of a hero. Since he has less and less time for everyday living, for the needs of his wife and children if he has them, he soon finds himself cut off and exiled from them. He feels abandoned by his family, whereas in fact he's the one who has abandoned them: he simply couldn't fit them into his work schedule.

Here we see the triumph of a mother complex that has managed to isolate an individual completely. By responding to his internalized ambitions, Bob has given in to the jealous, possessive love of an internal mother. Soon he won't be able to belong to anyone else at all. Hera protects her heroes, but she demands their absolute fidelity.

Why is it that so many priests, politicians, and evangelists get into trouble for sexual involvement with prostitutes or teenage boys? The reason is they can only express the instinctive sides of their natures surreptitiously.

Bob told me once that undergoing therapy made him feel as if he were doing something bad: he felt guilty about thinking his own thoughts by himself and for himself. He felt that constructing his own personal, individual world was a sin against nature. He confided that he couldn't write when his girlfriend was present, since he feared she would be able to guess his thoughts. "I can't seem to get far enough away from her," he confessed, but what he is really trying to get away from, of course, is his unconscious internal complex.

The hero belongs to society. He has never really been born, and his umbilical cord has never really been severed. All his actions are judged by an internal mother who can turn into a terrible witch if he doesn't find the strength to resist her. This is why personalities of this sort are so sensitive to criticism. A negative comment can wipe away their self-esteem in a few seconds and leave them feeling wounded for days. For heroes, the fear of criticism is their Achilles' heel.

The Obsession with Achievement

Bob the Hero is an excellent example of what we may call "loss of soul"; that is, for losing touch with emotions. Locked into the wonderful image of himself he has created, he quickly becomes a prisoner of the way others see him. In spite of his genuine accomplishments, he still has doubts about his masculine identity, and these doubts send him on a frantic quest for recognition. Unless he finds a significant father figure who can confirm him as a man—and this does occasionally happen—he will spend his whole life searching for his sense of identity. He will try to find it on the outside, in the eyes of others, because within him there is only emptiness and insecurity.

The hero idealizes his absent father; this gives the heroic son a taste for performance that knows no limits. Heroes evince a social ritual that eventually takes on religious overtones. Battalions of yuppies drag themselves to the office despite their utter exhaustion; they kill themselves with work, symbolically sacrificing their entrails on the altar of success. They are out to prove how capable they are, without ever asking who, if anybody, will benefit from it. Their attitudes have something excessive about them; one senses that they have lost touch with their inner selves and that deep within themselves they are terribly lonely.

For lack of appropriate outlets, this obsession with achievement at all costs expresses itself in other forms: obsession with "being worth a fortune"; with owning an expensive condo, a fancy house, and a number of cars. All these possessions cannot provide inner enjoyment, however, because they represent only substitute values, social camouflages, responses to the dictates of fashion. From deep within heroic men comes the cry, "I want to be recognized; I want my worth as a man to be confirmed by a father." Since we are social animals, this confirmation must come from an external moral authority. This is why the Catholic Church has made Confirmation a sacrament.

The frenetic behavior of the hero seeking a sense of self-worth is very similar to the way teenagers behave. In extreme cases, only the trauma resulting from some catastrophic event (such as burnout, a car accident, bankruptcy, divorce, an ulcer, or cancer) can put a stop to it. In all the mythologies, the gods provide severe punishments for heroes who go beyond the established limits or who commit the supreme crime of thinking themselves immortal.

All That Glitters Is Not Gold

In *The Fire from Within* by Carlos Castaneda,[1] the character Silvio Manuel remains always in the dark, never appearing in the light of day. As a teacher of the ancient art of the Yaqui sorcerers, he only speaks at night, in complete darkness, never seeing his listeners and never being seen by them. What a fascinating image this is—and how different from our own conception of the world! It is a restful image that comes into full focus when we compare it with expressions we use in our everyday language, expressions such as "to find a place in the sun," or "to seek out the limelight," or "to be in the spotlight."

We live with an exclusively solar mythology that has no place in it for the coolness of night. Going south for a winter tan—at the risk of developing skin cancer—has become a must for anybody who can afford "a place in the sun." We burn with ambition; we get sunburned on the beach; in short, we like the sun so much that we try to become it. We want to sparkle in the eyes of others. We want to become stars and, as Walter Pater put it, "to burn always with this hard, gemlike flame." Living in the shadows or existing in darkness has become a sign of mental illness for us. Therapists' offices are

---

1. Carlos Castaneda, *The Fire from Within* (New York: Simon and Schuster, 1984).

full of people suffering as a result of their inability to shine as brightly as others.

We know the legend of Icarus, who flew too close to the sun and was destroyed by it. His feathered wings, held together by beeswax, began to melt as he flew higher and higher, so that in the end he plummeted into the sea. This is the fate reserved for us when we become too "solar": we go down in flames, we experience burnout. Surely this is a graphic illustration of the symbol. We have given up our inner light for the light of recognition that comes only from the outside.

To avoid ending up like Icarus, we might follow his father's advice: fly neither too low nor too high. Heroes fly too close to the sun; tempting fate in that way brings about the downfall of the heroes' ideals of absolute perfection, of glory at any price. Incidentally, Jung said of the heroic son, "The sacrifice that signals the individual's separation from his mother also signals a renunciation of his own importance."[2]

Our fears and our shadows can become bridges to connect us to other people. Things we excel in, we can manage on our own, but it is our wounds and our weaknesses that help us communicate with others. We look for a shoulder to cry on or support from a friend only when we are troubled or upset. No one likes to face his fears alone. In this sense, the challenge for the hero is to let his real needs be seen by others.

The Impostor Complex

At the height of his career and in full possession of his abilities, Bob felt like an impostor. He suffered from a strange fear. Astonishingly, he was frightened that at any time he would be revealed as nothing but a fraud. With more than twenty years of acting experience behind him, he feared he would suddenly be unmasked and publically shown to have no theater knowledge or talent.

---

2. Carl Gustav Jung, *Symbols of Transformation, an Analysis of the Prelude to a Case of Schizophrenia, Collected Works*, vol. 5, 2nd ed., Bollingen Series XX. (Princeton, N.J.: Princeton University Press, 1967).

It requires enormous self-denial for an individual to achieve an exemplary career. The sacrifices made in the personal realm often rebound to the surface in the form of strange behavior and absurd, uncontrollable ideas. One of these ideas is the fear of being unmasked. This fear symbolizes the powerful identification of the individual with his social mask, his persona.[3] Though he forces himself to be pleasant and smiling in public, he finds himself filled with negative and aggressive feelings toward others; these feelings he cannot—or must not—let show. So he quite simply cuts himself off from all his inner life.

Feelings are our roots in life. They enable us to evaluate what is happening: is it agreeable or disagreeable, desirable or undesirable? Bob believes he is an impostor because he has lost touch with his personal truth. Only by getting in touch with his feelings can he regain a sense of wholeness. Bob isn't an impostor in his professional life, but he is one in terms of the overall development of his personality. That's the catch: overachievers' great fear is that people will notice the emptiness behind their public appearance. So overachievers throw themselves headlong into perfectionism as a way of hiding, or attempting to hide, their human weakness.

In the final analysis, negative feelings—the jarring notes in the social concert—perform the task of bringing us back to our unique and subjective reality. Returning to the world of his inner feelings allows a person to evaluate himself by himself. He can stop seeking others' evaluations of him. Sacrificing his perfection and acknowledging his human condition

---

3. The persona is the social mask we wear; it functions as a bridge between us and the external world. It represents a compromise between what we really are and the expectations the environment we function in has of us. Although the professor may identify with his own learning, and the policeman with his own power, if they are unable to remove their masks even in private, their whole personalities will suffer. The anima, whose role is to compensate for the persona, will be completely repressed, and the individual's inner life will diminish.

allows the individual to benefit from his talents himself and to be of benefit to others; he need not believe that his whole personality has always to be outstanding or exceptionally productive. The sudden anger or depression we glimpse behind a smile adds a dimension to the smiler, whom we might otherwise have dismissed as nothing but a phoney. The shadows give depth to a painting; things that are completely bright are suspect, and in the long run uninteresting.

Chariots of Fire

In his most common manifestation, the hero is not simply an idealist—far from it. He likes things that are showy and trendy, and he always comes equipped with various status symbols. Remember the ancient Romans and their fondness for chariots? Well, the fancy cars that parade through our towns and cities are in some ways modern versions of the ancient heroes' chariots in their processions of triumph. Everything about the hero is designed to have the right look.

Even the women or men the hero dates are part of his look. They are sexual symbols for those who admire the hero. They are used to arouse the envy of impotent voyeurs to whom the hero wishes to demonstrate his superiority. It's only fair to add that, although the hero may use his wife—if he has one—as a sexual object, she uses him as a success symbol. Certain women like men who are successful, and so whether he's a cultural star or the big man on Main Street, the hero never lacks female companions. Heroes arouse in these women the desire to be led away to the secret place where love can be consummated. Unfortunately, it's often no more than an illusion. Face-to-face contact often brings about the death of the hero; it means for him taking off his public mask and becoming just an ordinary person.

VINCE THE GOOD BOY

Vince is the kind of fellow who never raises his voice and is always careful to be kind and understanding. Even when people take advantage of him, he prefers to play the sucker rather than risk being unfair to someone. His main duty in life is to avoid doing anything that would make his mother cry. For Vince, making his mother cry is the cardinal sin. His deepest belief is: "I will get everything I want as long as I am nice, polite, courteous, and nonaggressive." His second duty in life is to let himself be trampled on as often as possible. His good reputation is tremendously important to him. If Vince walks down the street with a girl his mother wouldn't approve of, he feels ashamed of himself and hopes fervently that he won't meet anyone he knows. If he thinks he's going to have a confrontation tomorrow that might lead him to raise his voice, he won't be able to sleep tonight; he repeatedly rehearses the encounter in his head, going over and over the various ways he might handle the problem. He formulates the words he will speak, and learns them by heart.

The next night, if he has been brave enough to have the confrontation, he won't be able to sleep again. He's worried now that he raised his voice too much, and that he may have hurt someone or lost someone's respect. "My God, what if she never speaks to me again! What if she tells someone!" Then he tosses and turns in his bed, tormented by the most violent rejection fantasies; he tries to think of all the ways he can make amends. Looking full of confidence, but with his heart beating wildly, Vince meets his adversary the next day and flashes his warmest smile; it is a smile that says, "I didn't mean to hurt you, I'm really sorry, please forgive me. Mommy must never know about this."

If by any chance his silent plea is rejected, Vince puts the blame on the other person and takes refuge in anger. His rage allows him to cling to the brink of the precipice; it keeps him from falling into the gaping abyss of rejection. Alternately, feeling he has sinned against God and man, he punishes himself by sinking into a depression that temporarily takes away his enjoyment of life.

The good boy lives forever under the watchful gaze of

parents who are no longer present. He sees and interprets the new situations that come his way through the eyes of the child he was. It was after all in his childhood that he adopted the strategy of repressing any hint of revolt or aggrssivity that might have resulted for him, had he expressed it, in the pain of being deprived of his parents' affection. This strategy was a way of avoiding punishment, of ensuring he wouldn't be abandoned, of competing for love with his brothers and sisters. The more he was beaten, mistreated, or terrorized, the more he took refuge in passivity. He became what is known in psychoanalytic terms as a "passive-aggressive," passive and gentle on the surface, but angry and aggressive underneath.

Vince the Bad Boy

Luckily for Vince, the good boy has one characteristic that saves him from complete goodness: he almost always indulges in some hidden vice. Whether it's gambling, reckless driving, booze, pornography, stinginess, laziness, or overeating, there's usually one thing that doesn't quite fit with the rest of him, some little weakness he goes to great lengths to hide. Sooner or later, however, this little flaw will lead him into some situation which results in his losing face; this situation will be his chance to cast off the yoke of passivity and to finally, completely accept himself—even if that makes Mommy cry!

The only way Vince can deliberately get out of his predicament is his doing exactly what he fears to do: acting as he wishes and putting up with his guilt feelings—which are a necessary part of this process of self-affirmation. He has to learn to accept the fact that he may cause others to suffer. The good boy is particularly allergic to women's tears, and he often prefers to suffer himself rather than feel responsible for the suffering of others; this is his masochistic side. Nevertheless, in his dreams and his imagination, Vince sees himself as a veritable Superman, straight out of the movies, able to put everything right with a single scathing reply.

Vince the Really Bad Boy

The TV series "The Incredible Hulk" provides a fine illustration of the psychological makeup of the good boy. In his normal state, the Hulk is a good man who works wholeheartedly for the benefit of the community. He's a peace-loving man, the very model of kindness. If by any chance, however, he sees things turning against him, he is transformed into an incredibly ugly and terrifying monster who can tear a barroom apart in a few minutes and make short work of the bad guys.

The Hulk is like our good boy, Vince, who is also consumed by hidden rage. Vince's anger is usually expressed as sarcastic comments and cynical remarks, often directed against himself. Deep inside him, however, it's quite a different picture. Should Vince come up against an obvious lack of empathy and understanding, the volcano inside him explodes and the lava starts spewing out. He becomes vengeful, contemptuous, and bitter; he suddenly finds himself prey to a whole range of revenge fantasies, each one bloodier than the one before. Blackmail, deception—he can justify any means to attain his goals. Is this what it's all come to? Is this what he gets in return for his kindness? Is this all the thanks he gets for his efforts?

After a while Vince will no doubt try to control the evil thoughts that have come to him. If he still feels that everyone has abandoned him, he will wrap himself in a cloak of mystic sensibility, as if he were on the road to martyrdom.

Vince's relationship with his father is practically nonexistent. He pays back indifference with indifference. The good boy, it seems, has forgiven his father and has resigned himself to living in the world of his mother. He may in fact be quite comfortable in that world.

ERIC THE ETERNAL ADOLESCENT

We now move into a world whose outlines are soft and fuzzy. Eric is in his living room: amused, detached, ironic. He has a talent for making fun of everything, himself included, but he reserves his greatest scorn for yuppies and their perfect lifestyle. Chatting casually about the latest film he has seen, he sips at his coffee or beer, or rolls a joint. It's noon and he has just got out of bed. His hair is long and tangled, he hasn't shaved for three days. As he looks out the window he smiles condescendingly at the joggers struggling so hard to keep themselves in shape.

For Eric, society is a dark gray mass in which everybody has been homogenized and pigeonholed. This overly conventional society holds no interest for him. He has chosen not to work regularly for fear a steady job would clip his wings and diminish his precious freedom. He fears a steady relationship for the same reasons. All the girls he goes out with are nice, *but* . . . There's always a "but": but she's not interested in the arts, but she's got a kid, but her breasts are too small. Nothing is ever perfect enough for Eric to get totally involved in it. Living with a woman and having children with her would require a commitment he's just not ready for.

The eternal adolescent doesn't realize that he too is part of society, that in fact he is a quite recognizable cultural model. His appearance—cool, pleasant, and a bit unsure of himself—is a common male stereotype. Advertising companies profitably target this market of frightened bachelors who are trying to prolong their adolescence indefinitely.

At thirty-five, Eric still clings to the illusion that he can become anything he wants. He remains secretly convinced of his own genius and his own superiority, and he fantasizes about revealing himself to the world in some dazzling manner. He paddles around in a morass of dreams and fantasies from which he never extricates himself, and which he rather enjoys. Unlike the hero, he doesn't fight against his fusion with the unconscious; in fact, he revels in it.

Even though his imagination is something of a swamp, Eric is fascinated by heights: heights of inspiration, spiritual heights, mountain climbing, airplane flying, drug highs. You may find him prostrate before some great master or guru, in a state of enchantment that he hopes will never end. He is always searching for some ultimate revelation, some trip he'll never come down from. In this search he needs constant stimulation, and so he floats from girlfriend to girlfriend, from enthusiasm to enthusiasm, from treetop to treetop—like Tarzan. When reality intrudes and a fascination fades, the eternal adolescent crashes.

Eric lives in a world that is far-out, completely on the fringes. An ordinary person might decide to go to bed at two A.M. because he has had enough to drink and has to go to work in the morning; Eric will look down on him and automatically condemn him as straight, or a stick-in-the-mud. Whereas Bob the Hero lives in a world of high performance and achievement, Eric the eternal adolescent lives in the myth of whatever is cool.

There is another type of dormant eternal adolescent who never comes out into the open, so to speak. This type spends his life dreaming outlandish dreams that never amount to anything. He intends to write a great novel but never manages to put pen to paper. He wastes all his enthusiasm and energy daydreaming of success, yet he can never buckle down to anything requiring self-discipline. Sometimes he is deeply convinced that he will be the savior of humanity; he believes he is a divine being who will be spared from the ups and downs of ordinary life. He wants to be loved unconditionally for his potential, and he refuses to be assessed on the basis of his accomplishments. For him the tree is to be judged not for its fruit, but for its seeds and the promise they contain.

Rejecting a world in which love has to be earned, Eric represses his desire to make a breakthrough and leave his mark on the world. By so doing he castrates himself and cuts off his real creative potential. Living in an unreal world, he loses his grasp on reality, and this can have tragic consequences. Drugs and alcohol, which he uses as adjuncts to his creativity, may become crutches for his feelings of loneliness. They support not his creativity but only the banalities he desperately seeks to believe in. Then the adolescent, so full of promise, so full of magical talents with words and images, finds himself with his wings clipped for real. Drug and alcohol abuse transform him into a cynical and desperate old man who perceives the whole world through his narrow, pessimistic vision.

His attempt to escape from the world of his mother has been directed upward, in a rejection of the world of the flesh and life's necessary compromises. Of course, his attitude produces the exact opposite of its desired effect: Eric will never belong to any woman other than his mother and will never really be rooted in life. He will go on rejecting the realities of time and limits, just as he will go on denying the reality of his imperfections. His favorite song might well be the Beatles' tune, "Strawberry Fields Forever"!

Eternal Youth

Marie-Louise von Franz, the talented disciple of Jung, devoted an entire book to the problem of the eternal adolescent, entitled *Puer Aeternus*.[4] *Puer aeternus,* which is Latin for "eternal youth," is the name of an ancient god who possessed the ability to go on being endlessly reborn. In her book, von Franz includes a lengthy study of *The Little Prince* by Antoine de Saint-Exupéry. She invites us to think about the imaginary world in which the Little Prince lives; it is a solitary universe practically devoid of vegetation, a desertlike planet being devoured by a giant tree. Von Franz believes that this is the author's way of expressing his own inner solitude and his craving for feeling. Since the *puer* flees from real life and ends up living completely in his head, his world becomes dry and

---

4. Marie-Louise Von Franz, *Puer Aeternus: The Problem of the Puer Aeternus* (Zurich and New York: Spring Publications, 1970), p. 287ff. (The first part of this book is devoted to a study of *The Little Prince* by Saint-Exupéry. The information used in the following paragraphs is taken from pages 1–20.)

barren. The Little Prince yearns to be part of the world of the flesh; he wants to know the joys of flowers, of animals, and above all, of friendship.

Von Franz also demonstrates how Saint-Exupéry's mother complex is symbolized by the giant baobab tree that is devouring the planet on which the Little Prince lives. Furthermore, she shows how, all through his life, Saint-Exupéry could never adjust to everyday life on earth. He could never manage to spend more than a week or two at home with his wife; he was always in a hurry to get back to his plane and take off into the air. When he was declared too old to be a pilot, he used all sorts of schemes and ruses to gain another posting that would let him go on flying. As it turned out, this last assignment cost him his life, in 1944.

At the beginning of *The Little Prince*, Saint-Exupéry presents a sort of autobiography. He speaks in the first person of how his childhood drawings were not understood by the adults of that time any more than they are by the adults of today. He was never able to identify with the world of adults who were only interested in golf, bridge, and politics. He lived his whole life alone, never encountering an adult who could understand his sketches; the mysterious drawing that everybody took for a hat was in fact a boa constrictor that had swallowed an elephant.

Von Franz interprets this drawing as an obvious indication that the author's heroic self, symbolized by the elephant (an animal venerated for its strength and wisdom), was swallowed up by the mother, represented as a boa constrictor (which suffocates its victims). Saint-Exupéry did in fact have a mother who was very energetic and powerful. Independent observers have confirmed that it was difficult to resist the attraction of this woman's personality, and that she sometimes showed bizarre behavior. Whenever her son took off on a flying mission, for example, she would put on a black mantilla (a sign of mourning), since she always expected him to be killed! Von Franz states that in some cases, a son is driven to self-destructive behavior because of his mother complex, and that some mothers unconsciously long for their sons to die so that they can possess the sons eternally in death.

How Can Adults Remain Creative?

The fact remains that Saint-Exupéry had the creative power to write a number of masterpieces, and that he is considered a war hero and a pioneer in aviation. His problems appeared in other areas of his life. The eternal adolescent does not necessarily lack moral value or enthusiasm, but he is not able to integrate his creativity into his life as an adult. For him the two worlds of creativity and adulthood remain painfully incompatible. The character of the Little Prince represents Saint-Exupéry's artistic sensibility, which the author managed to preserve by taking refuge in sentimentality. This sentimentality represented his real contact with his deep individual self, and losing it would have been tantamount to suicide. His life and his work thus present us with the question how does one become an adult and at the same time preserve a childlike vitality and freshness of vision?

The *puer* represents the creative potential we all have within us. It is the part of us that cannot completely accept things staying the way they are. The *puer* goads us on, reminding us of our ambitions and encouraging us to dream. God knows, we do need to dream, for all our transformations of reality have their origin in dreams. But when the ego avoids undertaking to achieve these dreams and to integrate them into everyday reality, we become trapped in an eternal adolescence.

Are work, marriage, faithfulness, and discipline bitter but necessary medicines that will cure the eternal adolescent? A number of analysts, including Jung, believe so. However, James Hillman, an analyst who openly advocates the creative aspect of the *puer* psychology, maintains that Jung's is an excessively moralizing approach to the question, since by adopting it the individual risks losing the creative dimension that helps him to live.

Let us turn back to Eric the eternal adolescent. Although his chances of achieving his old dreams are greatly diminished, he is still obsessed with the idea of becoming a famous musician. During one of our therapy sessions he told me, rightly, that it didn't matter a damn to him what I, the therapist, thought; his ambition had kept him going and it was impossible for him to put it aside. One day when I dared express serious doubts about the possibility he would ever achieve his dream of fame and fortune, he put an abrupt stop to the therapy, storming out of my office and slamming no less than three doors on his way.

Another patient who, at the same age as Eric, was still living with his parents, came to consult me because a psychologist, after subjecting him to a whole battery of tests, had brutally told him he would never become an engineer because he clearly lacked the abilities. This patient simply needed someone to listen to him. After talking to me for an hour he announced, "In any case, I don't know if I've really got what it takes to earn that degree, but just the idea of the degree will help me get out of my parents' place and get a grip on my life."

Our dreams and our fantasies are charged with energy, and when we cut ourselves off from them we are depriving ourselves of vitality. James Hillman believes that the *puer* should be encouraged to do everything he can to actualize all his fantasies. If he wants to seduce a hundred women, let him go ahead! If he wants the whole world to worship him, let him give it a try! It is essential to encourage him to live in the real world, a strategy that has the advantage of not harming him as an individual.

PETER THE SEDUCER

With a smile that can be disarmingly timid or blatantly sexual, Peter exudes a charm that few can resist. He is a natural companion for Eric the eternal adolescent, and usually shares

Eric's dominant characteristics. Popular psychology explains his behavior with a stereotypical notion: he is looking for his mother in every woman he meets.

On closer examination, however, his attachment to the maternal world appears to be of a more complex nature. In general the seducer prefers the femme fatale. If his mother was tough, he will look for somebody gentle and understanding; if his mother was warm and emotional, he will seek a cold intellectual. The woman he is really after is the ideal mother he never had. He wants a woman who can fulfill all his desires, a woman whom he can worship as a goddess, a woman who will be simultaneously a mother, wife, and mistress.

Peter nonetheless often gets involved with women who basically resemble his mother. He becomes a victim of repetition, looking to women reminiscent of his mother for the things he never got from her, as if he would make up for some terrible emotional wound. If he needs tenderness he will not look for a sweet, gentle woman, but rather for one who is cold and reserved; then he can win her over and finally bring out the gentleness in her.

Peter's taste for love triangles also reveals a connection to his mother. He often finds himself attracted to women who are already attached, since the ones who are free frighten him. Competition seems to whet his appetite. His penchant for love triangles has its origin in the Oedipus drama: the seducer wants to supplant the father, escape from the father's authority, and take over the father's wife. However, the father still haunts him. For example, at the end of Molière's *Don Juan,* the great lover, after seducing more than two thousand women, must defend himself before the father of one of the girls he has seduced and abandoned.

Like Don Juan, Peter is capable of coldness, cruelty, and Machiavellian manipulations in order to reach his goals. This is his shadow, the dark, hidden side of what seems to be his warmth. Sometimes he loses all hope, and he barricades himself in his loveless world. Or else he sinks into cynicism as one woman after another succumbs to him and he gets bored with his own games. He blames his victims for their naïveté.[5]

That First Magic Moment

Peter's motives are not heroic but erotic. He flits from woman to woman, leaving each one in the lurch as soon as the novelty has worn off. He's supposed to be in love with love, but this doesn't entirely explain why he finds the early stages of a relationship so appealing. Could it be that this goes back to the very first moments of his life? Is the seducer trying to recreate that original moment of grace, when he lit up a woman's life by being born? Is he attempting to recapture the time when he was perfect and divine to his mother and she to him?

Since this recapturing is impossible to achieve, the seducer sets out to reconstruct the paradise of his life in the womb. In a sense he is trying to build what might be called a mystical uterus—*mystical* because it exists only in the mind and because the seducer's quest is basically religious, and *uterus* because women's sexual organs have become his most desired objects. They motivate his need to return to the very source of life.

The seducer constructs his temple so that it will be composed of the attributes and attitudes of all the different women he has seduced. He likes this one for her firm breasts, that one for her round buttocks and narrow vagina, another for her sharp mind, another because she's great company at a play or the movies. He loves Paula's conservatism. Michelle's voice really turns him on, and so forth.

Since he can never find a true, flesh-and-blood goddess, Peter creates one for himself using fragments of his various women. He is looking for a companion whom he can mold

---

5. I have adapted this concept of cynicism from Ginette Paris, who dealt with it in a lecture on Dionysius. Ginette Paris, "Le Masque de Dionysos" ("The Mask of Dionysius"), a lecture delivered to the C. G. Jung Circle of Montreal, May 13, 1988. (From my own notes taken during the lecture.)

according to his wishes, one in whom he can totally immerse himself. Fellini's film *Casanova* has a scene in which the aging lecher dances around a ballroom with a huge doll while his mother waves to him from the top of a long staircase. Finally he has found what he was after, a creature who fulfills all his aspirations: a mechanical doll. Women are objects for him, and incomplete objects at that. Each of his mistresses represents one fraction of a total moment—the magical moment he has pursued so ardently and for which he feels such existential nostalgia.

The Seducer as Victim

Why is it that women are so vulnerable to the charms of the seducer? To begin with, they love the intensity with which he pursues them; they are flattered by his passion and fine words; and they love all the delicate attention he showers on them. He is often able to zero in on each woman's uniqueness, that little something that other men don't seem aware of. He may discover a woman's hidden sense of humor, for example, or her taste for erotic games. He recognizes and reveals her individuality; he makes her feel feminine and beautiful. Each woman's unique, precious quality is precisely what the seducer is after. By the time he has won her over, though, and she thinks she has been accepted in the fullness of her being, he is already preparing to move on. He cherishes the memory of what he liked about her, but he is unwilling to commit himself to a relationship. So, often unwillingly, he breaks another heart—or breaks up another marriage.

Although our traditional moral values disapprove of a character like Peter, he nevertheless arouses our fascination and envy. These days a great many men and women have adopted his lifestyle. Their love affairs are brief and intense. Clearly this behavior implies a denial of the loved one's reality and a fear of committing oneself to a single exclusive relationship, but then why should marriage for life be considered the only viable model? Apart from considerations of the well-being of children, why should two people who no longer love one another be forced to go on living together?

At a broad social level, the role Peter plays in couples' breaking apart, or rediscovering their attachment to one another, shakes up the status quo. Although he is not aware of doing so, he fosters in many people a growing sense of their profound uniqueness; he is the source of their first real suffering or their first great joy. Peter is an agent of Eros, the winged god in constant motion, and he forces individuals to confront vital questions about love, passion, sex, and jealousy. What would life be, after all, without charm, without the worship of beauty? Basically it is a quest for the absolute, for what is *unique* in each person.

Seducers are generally highly sensitive individuals who refuse to accept their sensitivity. They cruise through life behind the protective shield of their seductiveness, until cynicism or the emptiness of their lives comes knocking on their door. The fragmentation of Peter's love affairs, the bits and pieces he collects are indicative of the fragmentation of his own being. In all his short-lived affairs and convoluted relationships, he is actually looking for his own wholeness. His cult of beauty is a step toward others; his passionate sensuality can move in new directions, revealing to him deep connections with the world, with trees and flowers and nature. If little by little this richer consciousness does develop within him, he may not have to end his life dancing with a mechanical doll beneath the enchanted gaze of his mother.

MICHAEL THE HOMOSEXUAL

Being Comfortable with Oneself

I hesitated a long time before including Michael in this rogues' gallery because his homosexuality is more than a lifestyle—it is a fact of nature. It is not something he chose or something he could easily change, like his work schedule or his number of sexual partners. His homosexuality simply came to him: he discovered his desire was directed toward men, and this discovery was as troubling to him as it was to those around him. It was all the more devastating because it potentially meant his life would be difficult and marginalized, plagued by the rejections and the sarcasms of heterosexuals. Michael could not choose to be a homosexual or not to be; his only real choice was whether or not to live his homosexuality openly.

I would like to depathologize Michael's sexual orientation. I certainly never felt that the goal of our therapy sessions was to turn him into a heterosexual. Psychology always seems to conceive homosexuality in developmental terms, as if it were acceptable only as a transitional stage on the way to heterosexuality—which is viewed as the only natural, normal condition. There seems to be problem in understanding that same-sex love and relationships are themselves complete and valid.

Having known a number of people who, like Michael, have shifted from heterosexual behavior to homosexual behavior, I have to conclude that the change often is highly beneficial to their sense of personal fulfilment. These people's homosexuality is not a proof of their immaturity; it is an integral part of their personal development. It appears they needed to undergo this experience in order to realize themselves fully. Homosexuality is every bit as valid as heterosexuality as a way of achieving selfhood. It may even serve as a stumbling block that differentiates an individual and launches him on his quest for individuation and freedom.

The debate on homosexuality gets off on the wrong foot when we conceive of sexuality in monolithic terms, as an existential condition, and when we fail to acknowledge that we all have desires and fantasies about people of our own sex. Homosexuality becomes a problem when we refuse to recognize our own homosexuality or homoerotic impulses, and when we project them outside ourselves. Our sexual energy moves between the two poles of heterosexuality and homosexuality; along this continuum, depending on the day, year, or period in our life, our orientation is more changeable than we may care to admit.

It is depressing to realize that more than forty years after the publication of the Kinsey Report, attitudes toward homosexuality have remained so hostile, despite the fact (or could it be because of the fact) that, as Kinsey's research showed, 37 percent of the American male population has engaged in homosexual behavior to ejaculation after the age of puberty?[6]

The most original part of Kinsey's study was the scale the researchers devised to measure sexual orientation, from exclusively heterosexual (0) to bisexual (3) to exclusively homosexual (6). The study was the first serious research project that did not treat homosexuality and bisexuality as pathological disorders but actually included them within the range of normal sexual behaviors. "The idea that sexual orientation is actually a *range* of behaviors and identities rather than a *condition*, that homosexuality is one of a number of normal variations in human sexual behavior, is one that Kinsey's numerous research studies have subsequently found to be both true and theoretically helpful in studying human sexual behavior."[7]

Anthropologists have discovered that homosexuality has existed in all human societies. This suggests a genetic predisposition in the attraction that one human being feels towards another of the same sex. The nature/nurture debate can never be fully resolved, though. In any case this debate is not the problem; the problem is the value judgements that we impose with regard to homosexuality. With both homosexuals and heterosexuals, the most important consideration is whether or not the individual is in conflict with his sexual orientation. If

6. Alfred Kinsey, Wardell Pomeroy, and Clyde E. Martin, *Sexual Behavior in the Human Male* (Philadelphia: W. B. Saunders, 1948), p. 625; quoted by Robert H. Hopcke, *Jung, Jungians, and Homosexuality* (Boston: Shambhala Publications, 1989), p. 4.

7. Hopcke, *Jung, Jungians,* p. 4.

a person is in harmony with himself, if he feels comfortable about who he is, I see no reason for psychology to reproach him.

The bias against homosexuals is all the more astonishing when one considers the tremendous contributions they have made to past and present societies. As Robert H. Hopcke notes in his book *Jung, Jungians and Homosexuality*, homosexuals were very highly regarded in a number of Amerindian tribes; "men-women" or "women-men" called *berdaches* were actively sought as companions; a berdache often held a central position in the tribe, sometimes even the position of chief.

Certain psychological conditions nevertheless have a great influence on the polarization of the sexual libido. I intend therefore to look at how the father's absence has affected Michael's behavior, and especially at how the missing father may have stimulated Michael's homosexual libido; let me stress once again that I consider this libido to be perfectly natural. The point I wish to make is that a homosexual orientation of the libido depends less on an attachment to the mother than on a search for the missing father. Attachment to the mother certainly exists among homosexual men, and since the whole family system is involved, this attachment is that much stronger in cases in which the father is inadequate.

I should make it clear that mine is a psychological interpretation of this phenomenon and as such is necessarily reductive; although it cannot account for the entire phenomenon of homosexuality, it can reinsert homosexuality into the contexts of masculinity and father-son relationships. Whether we are homosexual or heterosexual, our behaviors are rooted in our own psychological, familial situations, which humanize, actualize, and orient for us the great archetypal energies. Problems arise when certain attitudes or behavior become rigid, repetitive, or destructive of our individual well-being. A compulsive need to seduce, which stems from a fear of emptiness and abandonment, is an example of such a problem. There are pathological forms of homosexual behavior just as there are pathological forms of heterosexual behavior; neither orientation prevents problems, despite what many heterosexuals would like to believe.

Sexual Awakening

I am often struck by the kinds of experiences that lead to sexual awakening for gay men. Often the first homosexual experience occurs at a critical moment in childhood or puberty. This experience can have a determining effect on a boy's entire sexual development.

For example, Paul's mother died in childbirth. When Paul was still very young, his father, overwhelmed by caring for his many children, sent his son to live with an uncle. There Paul shared a bed with a very affectionate cousin, and soon his need for love became eroticized. Henry, another of my patients, was placed in a foster home with a couple he thought were his grandparents. He had been told his father was in the Air Force, and he found himself attracted to soldiers. They would sometimes share his bed.

For the adolescent boy, homosexual behavior is often motivated by the need to explore the male body in order to root himself in masculinity. In many cases it is simply a transition period. At this age the guys he hangs out with are tremendously important to a boy. Many males are particularly vulnerable at this stage. They are transferring their identification from women to men. Making this change renders male identity quite fragile. Homosexuality can become a refuge at this stage; when the father is absent and there are no adequate paternal substitutes, some boys will lack the necessary support to make a secure identification transfer and will thus remain identified with the feminine element.

The Need for Initiation by the Father

Jung interprets homosexuality[8] as an identification with the anima (the feminine component). This interpretation would

---

8. Carl Gustav Jung, *Psychological Types,* Collected Works, vol. 6, Bollingen

explain why some homosexuals adopt "feminine" mannerisms. An identification with the anima automatically causes an individual to look for his own (masculine) persona in someone of the same sex. It also accounts for some homosexuals' fascination with typically masculine objects, such as chains, boots, or military uniforms. It explains why some men like sadomasochistic scenes and leather bars, where they can play at being "real" men. Anthony Stevens sees this phenomenon as indicating an unconscious desire for initiation; it is a search for a stern, strong father, and the search takes place in the areas of sex and seduction.[9] Both Jung's and Stevens's interpretations shed light on forms of behavior that might otherwise seem absurd to the uninitiated.

Michael, who is forty, heads a young company he founded; he has struggled hard to keep it growing and ahead of the competition. He told me about the following incident, which had happened several times and which had totally unnerved him: he was having lunch with several older businessmen and at some point during the meal he felt an unaccountable urge to say, "You know, I'm not a real businessman." One of the other businessmen was a banker from whom Michael was trying to get a loan for $100,000, and the others are very important customers of Michael's. A statement like Michael's was almost a sure recipe for disaster! Every time this incident happened, Michael returned to his office in tears, stunned by his self-destructive actions. What on earth could account for his strange compulsion?

If we look at Michael's behavior as showing a need to be initiated by the father, then it becomes much easier to understand. Actually, by expressing his vulnerability to businessmen older and more experienced than himself, he reinforces them as strong father figures. He ensures he will get a response like

---

Series XX, 2nd ed. (Princeton, N.J.: Princeton University Press, 1967), pp. 471–472.
    9. Stevens, *Archetypes*, p. 172.

"Sure you are a real businessman; you're doing really well!" Such a response makes him feel accepted into the community of men, elevated to the same level as them, and initiated into his own masculinity.

Behavior similar to Michael's compulsion appears in sado-masochistic relationships, in which one partner plays the role of dominator and the other of victim. Through a game of mutual projections, the one initiates the other into the mysteries of masculine power, and vice versa. Such initiation, however, is limited by its restriction to sexual behavior; it thus must be repeated with each resurgence of sexual desire.

Freud too believed that the father's absence plays a central role in orienting sexual identity. In his study of Leonardo da Vinci he notes that the excessive affections of his mother, who had been abandoned by her husband, spurred the young genius to identify with the feminine. A child must choose between keeping his love for himself or investing it in a person of the opposite sex. Freud saw homosexuality as a compromise between keeping one's libido for oneself and yielding it to someone else. Indeed, absolute self-love, or primary narcissism, is an essential development phase for all of us, during which we believe ourselves to be the center of the world. It is severely shaken by the individual's discovery of the difference between the sexes. The shock of this discovery can be healed and self-esteem restored through admiration of the parent of the same sex, but only providing that the parent reciprocates with a similar admiration. When the father is absent this mutual admiration is not available to the boy. The boy is left uncertain of his identity and remains frightened of sexual difference.

It might be claimed that some homosexuals use their homosexuality to attempt to suppress the reality of sexual difference, in order to remain in sameness, in what most resembles themselves. To some degree they are in the same position as seducers, who also have trouble accepting otherness. Many homosexuals, like the Don Juan types, frequently change partners. This ensures that the loved one will remain present only as long as the desire or fantasy endures. It ensures that the loved one's reality will never have a chance to intrude on those desires and fantasies.

Both Freudian and Jungian interpretations can be criticized for the lack of flexibility in the way they view homosexuality. In this regard, I would like to draw the reader's attention to Robert H. Hopcke's book *Jung, Jungians, and Homosexuality*, cited earlier. A gay psychotherapist himself, Hopcke uses analytical psychology to form a practical, open, and nonmoralistic conception of human sexuality. He maintains that each person, male or female, is influenced internally by the major currents of male, female, and androgynous energy. This focus on the androgynous element adds a new dimension to the debate on homosexuality. It leads Hopcke to conclude that there can never be a general explanation for individual sexuality, which is always the fruit of the intermingling and interplay of these three archetypal forces according to the circumstances of each person's life. Hopcke's theories thus move away from overly rigid conceptions of sexual orientation, as is apparent in the following passage dealing with bisexuality.

> *If all sexual orientation is the result of a personal and archetypal confluence of the masculine, feminine, and Androgyne, then bisexual men and women are not strange creatures, sexual anomalies, outsiders, fence sitters, but individuals whose masculine, feminine, and androgynous energies merge and flow in a particular pattern in response to certain archetypal and personal experiences. Such a theory also permits one to understand how an individual's sexual orientation might change over the course of a lifetime, from adolescence to young adulthood to middle age and beyond, and provide a way to look at who and what has shifted in the life of the individual.*[10]

---

10. Hopcke, *Jung, Jungians*, p. 187.

Reclaiming the Body

Michael has not always been active as a homosexual. In his twenties he lived with a woman for several years. His life was then profoundly shattered by his first homosexual experience. His mother was a dominating woman who had a fierce temper and, as Michael put it, "something crazy about her." When he was a teenager, he had trouble getting along with his father, and that left him with a wounded sense of masculinity. So he took off into the air. He became one of those flighty creatures who seem to float through life, seemingly always easygoing and somewhat detached.

His relationship with his girlfriend had been warm and open. During their sexual relations, however, he could reach a climax only after performing a lot of mental contortions. Everything took place in his head rather than in his body, and he would have to imagine all sorts of things in order to maintain an erection. He characterizes his homosexual relations as "more electric" and "more physical": the pleasure was no longer just in his head, but throughout his whole body, and the physical contact with his partner was positively reinforced.

These brief observations bring us to the heart of the problem. What we see from Michael's experience is that, basically, his relationships with men give him access to his own body. His absent father and his difficult mother caused him to feel embarrassed by his body. These feelings became particularly powerful when he was in contact with a woman. He feared letting himself go and giving in completely to physical pleasure; he remained an observer during his own sexual activities.

Michael speaks of gay sex as if it were a ritual through which he can recover possession of his body and emotions. He generally chooses passive partners who are dependent upon him. This gives him the chance to do something that will raise his self-esteem: he is the protagonist playing the active role, the one who arouses sexual excitement. His partners enable him to declare, "I am not my mother!" Gay sex enables him to tear himself away from his mother's body and regain access to his own vitality. In my opinion, this repossession of the body and rediscovery of sensitivity are at the core of many homosexual relationships.

When a man has suffered from the physical and emotional absence of his father, it is not surprising that he should attempt to rediscover himself through a physical exploration of the male body. Some kinds of things can be learned only from those of the same sex. For example, a little girl trying to put on makeup for the first time would not likely ask a man for help. The same are at work in the endless contests young boys indulge in to develop their heroism. They constantly measure themselves against one another; they even compare the size of their penises. This is a reality of the male condition, a necessary step in male development.

The affective presence of the father enables a young man to experience his own body as something beautiful that he can inhabit with pride. The majority of homosexuals have had terrible experiences with their fathers; it is through gay sex that a gay man claims the right to love the male body, beginning with his own. Most men, homosexuals and heterosexuals alike, do not consider they have the right to find themselves beautiful. One of my gay patients did not look for sexual pleasure with his lovers—he simply wanted to draw their hands and bodies over and over again. His art was a celebration of the male body.

The basis of an individual's identity takes root in a body similar to his own. This no doubt explains why a lot of gay men work out so often in fitness clubs: they are unconsciously starting over from the very beginning, at the point at which something went wrong. When someone does not feel good about himself, the first thing he thinks to do is to change his body: a new hair style, or a new outfit, or even plastic surgery for the nose or the jaw. Similarly, a young man often "becomes" gay because another man—often the first one who did so—found him beautiful, desired him, and gave him some much-needed attention.

Fear of Women

As is also true of many heterosexual men I will speak of later, Michael's fear of what is radically different from himself is focused in his fear of the female sex organs. He is not frightened of women as friends or companions; what frightens him is the natural woman herself, the woman with a body and a vagina. This fear may also indicate Michael's attachment to his mother since, curiously, the mother's vagina remains the great unknown in the child's relationship with her. Without realizing it, Michael is obeying a decree that he must never belong to any other woman.

On the other hand, Michael compensates for this with an almost religious devotion to famous movie stars like Marilyn Monroe or Greta Garbo. This veneration of the woman as goddess reflects his fascination with the image of the mother, an image he would like to keep forever perfect and adorned with all the attributes of divinity. Like his own mother, these superstars are untouchable for Michael. That suits him just fine, since he doesn't want to touch women anyway.

Many homosexuals report having witnessed scenes of violence between their parents, or having seen their mothers beaten by their fathers. How could they respect their own sex after seeing such scenes? Such a son assumes the role of protective guardian of the mother in emotional trouble, and this intensification of his links with his mother's body heightens his fears of being devoured and of touching another woman.

Homoeroticism

The homosexual gets caught up in the same dilemma as the heterosexual in that he too is driven by the idea of finding the perfect partner—someone with whom he can share a lasting relationship. Perhaps because there are rarely children involved, or because the illusion of the ideal couple is often just that, many gay men tend, though, to drift from one short-lived affair to another; they move from total infatuation to complete disillusionment in the space of a few months. Every time one of my patients is going through this process, I keep hoping, along with him, that this relationship will turn out to be the right one. We both know, though, that there's a good chance it won't work out: being too much in love, or wanting too much to be in love, basically means not having enough love for oneself.

I sometimes think that Michael is looking not so much for sex as for a kind of eroticism. Even as adults, many men feel a deep need to be with others of their own sex. A number of the men's groups with which I have been involved have been eloquent on this point: getting together makes them more sure of themselves, more confident and dynamic. They say it makes them less wary of other men. Quite simply, they discover their need for homoerotic relationships: their need to share feelings and affection with other men. The very fact of seeing other men express their vulnerability or their violence, the very fact of talking with each other and touching each other, confirms their own identities as men. In every man there is a homoerotic component that he must recognize if he wants to develop fully as a human being. As Hopcke points out, we have to learn to celebrate diversity instead of seeing it as something pathological.

JULIAN THE FEMINIST

Like a lot of men of his generation, Julian went through a feminist period. He read Germaine Greer and several volumes of Anaïs Nin's diaries; he studied the essays of Simone de Beauvoir, and he was enthusiastic about Doris Lessing's *Golden Notebook*. In the wave of cultural upheavals that swept over the world in the late sixties, Julian became a feminist. In theory, he still is. What were his real motives in embracing feminism? Could it be that he used feminism as just another way of ingratiating himself with women?

Julian is now thirty years old. He was particularly close to his mother, who suffered from depression and from abuse by her authoritarian husband. When Julian was a teenager, his defense of his mother led to several confrontations with his father. These experiences in his childhood and adolescence made it difficult for him to identify with the masculine, and also made him particularly sensitive to the concerns of women. He was a feminist before the feminist movement existed. Julian married a strong, intelligent woman and shared her ideas about how their life as a couple should work. Then came the first baby. There were very few hitches during the pregnancy, although Julian felt increasingly abandoned. Once the child was born, however, things went much less smoothly. Julian couldn't cope with his wife giving all her attention to the baby. Since he couldn't get her to take his frustrations seriously, he became violent.

What happened to Julian happens to a lot of men. As soon as they lose the full attention of their companion, they feel like they no longer exist. Their world crumbles and they fall into the void. They become children again, bad tempered and capricious. For the woman, it is like having one more kid on her hands.

The deep reason for Julian's involvement with feminism lies in his fear of being abandoned and in his intense desire to be rewarded with maternal affection for even his smallest acts on behalf of women. His feminism does not come from a conscious decision; it is only another attempt to please women and to stay in their good graces. As long as a man is not liberated from his mother he cannot love another woman; his libido, his vital force, remains imprisoned in his mother complex. He is not able to sacrifice his own needs in order to respond to the needs of another.

All too often, men cheat on their wives or leave them either when they are pregnant or just after they have given birth: at the very times when the women have the greatest need of their husbands' presence and support. In this way the tradition of absent fathers perpetuates itself.

Feminism is the result of women thinking long and hard about their condition as women. It calls for us not to accept it blindly, but rather for us to think equally long and hard about our own condition as men. Superficial feminist men are really no more than "Mommy's boys" who cannot completely hide their deep fear of women.

NARCISSUS, WOUNDED IN LOVE

Echoes of Marie

I was sitting in a bar, having a beer with Marie, a woman about my age whom I knew from work. It had been months since we'd seen one another and we had a lot of catching up to do. With the arrival in the bar of a certain good-looking young man, however, our conversation took a very unexpected turn. He had barely set foot in the place when Marie started choking on her drink. I asked what was wrong. She then proceeded to tell me about the bizarre experience she had had with him.

In the course of the previous summer Marie had taken a fancy to the young man in question, who was eight years younger than her. She had been attracted by his charm, and especially by his irresistible smile. For the first little while they had a very pleasant relationship, but after going out with him for just a few months she began to sense a tremendous emptiness in their relationship: it was as though he was only interested in his own reality. He insisted on being the center of attention, and he turned everything to himself. If Marie started to tell something personal about herself, he would interrupt with something similar that had happened to him. He showed interest in what she was doing only when he could profit from it directly. It seemed as though there was no room for her in his life.

One day when Marie was about to deliver an important lecture, he started quarreling with her about something insignificant just minutes before her presentation. He seemed to take great pleasure in spoiling her enjoyment of things; it was as if he couldn't tolerate her pleasure or success unless it depended on him. She always had to take a back seat to him or pretend he was the center of her universe; otherwise, their relationship didn't work.

At the feeling level, things were not much better. The young man had trouble opening up and letting himself be touched. He was all wrapped up in himself and showed little trust in other people. Still, every time Marie decided to leave him, he would cling to her and protest vehemently. It just didn't make sense. Marie concluded he was interested in her for her money and reputation; he was more attracted by what she had and did than by who she was. He didn't care about *her*—all he cared about was having someone to lean on.

Instead of running away, Marie dug in her heels. She wanted to discover her lover's secret, and her discreet enquiries quickly led in the direction of his childhood. She thought his behavior stemmed from his having been spoiled as a child, from his parents catering to his every whim. Much to her surprise, though, Marie found the real situation to have been quite different. It was true he had never lacked for anything in a material sense, and his parents had given him a lot of attention. All that had been done, however, in order to fill him with their own ambitions, with no respect for his own individuality. This explained why, although he had a university degree, he always preferred jobs outside his area of specialization. He had earned his diploma to please his parents; now that he had it, he steered as far away as he could from any of their desires for him.

Marie came to understand that her friend's parents had never recognized him as a completely distinct person. This was why he was always trying to impose himself on her: he was suffering from wounded love. His wound was so deep that he couldn't risk exposing it. When Marie attempted to breach the subject with him, he refused to say anything. He could not stand seeing his own vulnerability reflected in the eyes of another; he needed a lover who would believe in him absolutely. Marie was becoming too negative a mirror. He lived to be desired, he said, not to be criticized. He quickly lost interest in Marie and left her, without ever understanding her attachment to him.

The encounter in the bar was the first time he and Marie had met after several months of separation. I sensed that Marie wanted to talk with him, so I left her there with him. On my way home I started thinking of the myth of Narcissus, the young man who refuses the advances of beautiful Echo, and falls in love instead with his own reflection. I decided Narcissus would be a good nickname for Marie's lover.

To Be Desired at All Costs

Contrary to what we might think, Narcissus does not love himself too much or love only himself. Rather he suffers from a terrible lack of love because he didn't get enough of it as a child—at least not enough to give him confidence in himself and make him feel worthy of the respect of others. His intrinsic individuality and his uniqueness as a person were not sufficiently recognized in his family environment. His search for love today is fierce and consuming, especially because it is largely unconscious. His strategy, to please at all costs, attempts to fill up the void within him.

Psychoanalysts use this myth of Narcissus falling in love with his own reflection as a metaphor for the narcissistic personality[11] using other people to mirror itself, seeking a

---

11. In its most serious aspects the psychology of the lost son is strikingly similar to the narcissistic behavior examined by neo-Freudian psychoanalysis. See, for example, the brilliant studies of Heinz Kohut, *The Analysis of the Self*

glimmer of recognition in their eyes. Narcissus lives only to be desired.

To be desired! Is this not the same ambition as that of the hero, the seducer, the *puer*, the homosexual, the young father who is jealous of all the attention his wife gives to the baby? What's wrong with wanting to be desired? Nothing, but a problem does arise when an individual is so driven by this need that he loses sight of his own nature, his own limits and imperfections—like Narcissus in the myth, who drowns in his own reflection.

In order to be desired, Narcissus has to mold himself in accordance with another person's desire. This can cause him to develop a false self, and become overadapted to his environment. As a result of this process, Narcissus will be tense, uptight, and unable to let himself go—as if he feared punishment for straying from the standards of acceptability.

Narcissus finds confirmation of his own being in the eyes of others. Other people act as mirrors for him, corroborating the fact that he exists. The closer he gets to people he considers important, the more important he feels himself. He loves the company of prominent people. As Marie pointed out, he likes to hang out with these people, but what he is really doing is hanging on to them.

Narcissus will never admit his desperate need for others, since doing so would force him to acknowledge the emptiness inside him. The less he feels on the inside, the more frantic and hopeless his search for understanding and affection will become. His happiness and sense of identity depend exclusively on being popular and well liked. In fact, it is this very exclusive dependency that gets him into trouble.

(New York: International Universities Press, 1971); and *The Restoration of the Self* (New York: International Universities Press, 1977). This psychology of narcissism connects with the psychology of the *puer* described by analytic psychology (Jungian). It is also related to what is generally called the "passive-aggressive character."

Narcissus's self-confidence fluctuates enormously, rising if he looks good in the mirror of the eyes of others, falling if the image he sees there is unflattering. He is extremely vulnerable to negative criticism and responds to it with self-loathing. He is unable to like himself or feel proud of his accomplishments, and he even has trouble taking credit for his real achievements. The reflections he sees in the mirror inside him are highly disparaging. An inner voice is constantly whispering, "That's not enough! You're no good! Do better!"

Narcissus has become an important figure in our culture, as is made clear in the book by the historian Christopher Lasch, *The Culture of Narcissism*.[12] A narcissistic culture is essentially based on the notions of success and failure. It does not recognize anything in between. In such a culture images are tremendously powerful: what you look like is more important than what you are. Such a society suffers from too great an identification with the persona, that is, the social mask. The emphasis on self-image necessarily leads to a handicapping of the overall development of the personality of the individual, at the expense of the anima, which soon becomes the madwoman in the attic.

ROCK THE REBEL

In Search for the Missing Father

In the winter of 1988, Canadian television presented a five-hour-long miniseries entitled *Rock*. The series described how a teenage boy ran away from his home in a rural Quebec village and headed for Montreal in search of his father. Disillusioned and short of money, the boy soon turned to petty theft and prostitution before the police finally picked him up. Rock was

---

12. Christopher Lasch, *The Culture of Narcissism: American Life in an Age of Diminishing Expectations* (New York: Warner Books, 1979), p. 447.

placed in a home for juvenile offenders and was eventually rehabilitated. The childhood friend who had run away with Rock was less fortunate; he ended up in prison and turned into a hardened criminal. After his release he got into a fight with his father and stabbed him, almost killing the man.

The near-murder of a father by his own son was an appropriate ending for the series, which dealt with the problem of absent fathers. Rock's father had in fact disappeared without warning, leaving his family and his business behind. His was the old story of going out to buy a pack of cigarettes and never being seen again. Rock couldn't accept the fact that his father had deserted them, and he was very troubled when his mother started a new life with another man.

In a very moving scene that happens just before Rock decides to take off for the city, he goes down to the village port in the hope of hearing news of his missing father, who had worked as a sailor. On this day a boat captain, his father's friend and messenger, has a parcel for Rock; it contains a gold-colored lighter and a cassette. Wild with anticipation, the youth runs to the top of a cliff beside the sea and prepares to listen to the message he has been waiting for all this time. He thinks he is about to learn the real reasons for his father's departure, and he also hopes to hear his father is coming back. Rock sets his ghetto blaster on a stone and settles back to listen. The father's message is confused, incoherent, and banal, though, and filled with long periods of silence.

Bitterly disappointed and half-crazy with frustration, Rock finally yells out, "Talk, for chrissake, just say it!" Then he gives the tape recorder a violent kick and sends it tumbling into the sea. This scene is followed by a mad race through the forest; Rock grabs a maple sapling and tears it up by its roots. This act is a symbol of the uprooting and destruction of Rock's young life. His father's desertion and silence will lead Rock into the hell of juvenile delinquency, as he searches for the missing man.

Untamed Energy

Juvenile delinquents are gangs of young rebels who have become involved with alcohol, prostitution, or drugs, and who live on the street. Hanging out on the street becomes natural to them; so does living in poverty and being sick. Their delinquency shows what can happen when the turbulent energy of youth remains untamed and unchannelled by the father's presence. Out of revenge or out of the simple need to survive, they go about causing harm—as a reaction to the harm that has been done to them. Delinquents are our negative redeemers: they remind us of our own imperfect humanity, which we tend to lose sight of in the midst of all our idealistic preoccupations.

It is interesting to note that these juvenile gangs reproduce the very order they are rebelling against. They demonstrate a surprising level of hierarchy and discipline; they obey gang members who have committed the most serious offenses, the ones who have risked their lives, or those who have spent time in prison. A number of these gangs also have initiation rites that are reminiscent of traditional rituals. Some motorcycle clubs, for instance, require their followers to have killed someone before they can be admitted as full-fledged members. Other gangs make new members urinate on a leather jacket or rape a woman. In all instances an initiate must demonstrate his strength and his willingness to act "like a man." Heroism, loyalty, and solidarity are all promoted, to the point where a member can only quit the gang at the risk of being killed.

The Evil Father

The problem of delinquency is more widespread than is usually realized. Gangs of heavily armed adolescents actually go to war against one another for control of drug markets. In the city of Los Angeles alone, in 1987 there were more than 400 murders resulting from battles between rival street gangs, and it is estimated that there are more than 70,000 gang members in some 600 different groups in that city.[13] In Canada the activities of some motorcycle gangs came to light with the discovery in 1986 of eight bodies in the St. Lawrence River, all wrapped in sleeping bags and weighted down with cement blocks. This massacre also turned out to be drug related; two gangs had been battling for control of the same territory.

Names like Hell's Angels or Satan's Choice refer more or less directly to the figure of the Evil Father. Anything to get closer to the father! Sons who do not seek the Heavenly Father may end up in the clutches of the Father of Hell. This can be seen as the resurgence of a primitive force in which the opposites good and evil remain divided.

Individuality involves the ability to reconcile these opposites within oneself. Being both good and bad, strong and weak, the adequate father shows his son what it is to be human. If he has not revealed his personal humanity to his child, a father condemns his son to modelling himself on stereotypical, macho images involving absolute obedience, power struggles, and contempt for women. The son falls prey to uncontrollable aggressive impulses, and he will go to any lengths—even murder—to prove his virility.

DESPERATE FRED

Fred was a tall, muscular, and sensitive young man who was sent to me by one of his professors. Fred seemed to me unusually cynical and sarcastic. He was also a brilliant student, having finished his B.A. at the age of twenty. The first thing he told me was that he didn't know what he was doing there in my office. He was so nervous he couldn't sit still; he kept getting up, turning his back to me, and going over to the window. On his wrist I could see the swollen scar left by the blade he had slashed himself with the previous month.

13. Based on a Canadian Broadcasting Corporation radio news report, April 3, 1988.

Meaningless Pain

Like Fred, more and more young people are trying to put a quick end to their lives. For this age group, suicide has now become the leading cause of death, except for car accidents. The problem has reached epidemic proportions, and it shows every sign of increasing in frequency with each new generation.

In France, the statistics on suicide show a dramatic change in recent years. Up until 1975, more men over forty committed suicide than those in the twenty-to-forty range. Since 1975, however, the suicide rate for young men has been higher than for the older ones. In addition, the actual number of suicides in young people has increased dramatically: 12,500 in 1985 compared to 8,300 in 1975.[14]

The Canadian province of Quebec holds the unfortunate distinction of having the world's highest number of suicides for young people between eighteen and twenty-five. In the pre-university age group, one out of every twelve students admits to having attempted suicide, and in 1982 alone there were 421 suicides in the under-thirty age group.[15] Successful attempts were twice as frequent for males as for females.

Suicide, the famous study by Emile Durkheim, published in 1897, revealed the fact that people do not commit suicide simply because of mental health problems: suicide also has social causes. Societies to which people have a strong sense of belonging show the lowest rates of suicide; as the norms governing social order disintegrate, suicide rates increase.

Older generations were able to handle the pressures of living in precarious financial circumstances, but the more affluent young people of today have given up hope. The older genera-

---

14. Alain Philippe, *Suicide, évolution actuelle* (Suicide, the Situation Now), (Paris: Interforum, 1988).

15. "Le suicide chez les jeunes prévenu grâce à un video" (Teenage Suicide Prevention, Thanks to a Video), (*La Presse,* Montreal, 1987).

tions' religious faith, their belief in progress and future material comfort, and the possibility of providing an education for their children all gave meaning to their sacrifices. Now, however, with unemployment threatening in all walks of life, with the increase of stress in the modern world, and with the erosion of old traditions, there seems for young people to be no meaning to life.

According to a survey conducted by the mental health department of a Montreal hospital, young people turn to suicide as a way of *putting a stop to their pain*. The pain that Fred feels, the pain that afflicts a person's entire being, is pain with no apparent meaning: suffering with no obvious explanation. Again, the father's absence has brutal repercussions indeed.

The role of the father in tribal initiation rites is to give meaning to suffering. The mutilations that fathers perform upon their sons is an integral part of the ritual. Young men learn to withstand pain, to tame it and master it, so they can gain admittance to the world of men. The wounds deliberately inflicted by fathers symbolize life's suffering and give it a mythic significance. Suffering goes hand in hand with the development of a young person's being and of his experience of the laws of the universe.

Today, in our culture, the meaning of suffering has been lost. It is no longer transmitted by fathers; in their obsession with comfort, they now use any means they can to avoid suffering (including the very common means of abandoning their wives and children). When the role of suffering is not understood—and not transmitted by the father—we are confronted with the sad spectacle of a generation of young people trying to run away from the horrors of the world, and taking refuge in suicide. Suicide is the most radical action a human being can take to escape the pain of living and to conquer the absurdities of existence.

CHRIS THE ADDICT

Instant Illumination

Chris is a survivor of substance abuse. He is forty years old. A child of the baby boom, he grew up in the midst of postwar economic prosperity and the countercultural revolution. Drugs accompanied his cultural initiation rites. His cultural gurus were the Beatles, Marcuse, and Dr. Timothy Leary, the high priest of LSD. Chris rejected the values of his father, who was a drinker.

For Chris, drugs were a way to make contact with infinity. By altering his perceptions, they provided him with instant access to new states of consciousness that in turn revealed to him different approaches to the structures of the world and the psyche. At twenty, Chris was a true son of Dionysus.

The Master of Transformations

In Greek mythology Dionysus is the god of ecstasy and intoxication; he presides over initiations and transformations. A precursor of Christ, he too died only to be born again. He was killed and dismembered by disciples who then ate his flesh; afterwards, his nymphs reassembled the parts of his body. This rite symbolizes intoxication by alcohol: under its influence the drinker falls into pieces, but when he wakes up afterwards he can pull himself together again. The Christian mystery of transubstantiation has maintained some elements of Dionysian ritual, such as the priest's drinking wine in the Mass.

In most initiation rites, neophytes are invited to take part in certain exercises or to ingest certain substances that will entrance them: any metamorphosis requires a suspension of ordinary consciousness. These rites put the novice in contact with superhuman elements, with the life or spirit that lies hidden behind ordinary appearances. Alcohol is called *spirits* and fine brandies are called *eaux-de-vie* ("water of life"). Hallucinogenic mushrooms are called *magic* mushrooms, and cannabis is sometimes called *the devil's weed.*

For the followers of Dionysus, the bacchanal was a feast that encouraged all kinds of excesses: debauchery, orgies, dances, drunkenness. It was a celebration of the god, an attempt to enter into his spirit and partake of his ecstasy. Like our modern-day carnivals (of which it is the ancestor), the ritual bacchanal took place at prescribed times of the year. Nowadays we have lost touch with the real meaning of the bacchanal as a special time; instead, we celebrate indiscriminately all year long. We expect perpetual pleasure, and we refuse to wean ourselves from it. No surprise then that what now emerges is the god's darker side; instead of transforming us, our bacchanals are much more likely to fix us in permanent immaturity.

When you consider how many thousands of baby boomers shared Chris's unquenchable thirst for magic potions, it is hard not to conclude that there was actually a self-destructive impulse in their quest for change at all costs. Any Dionysian metamorphosis includes the mystery of death, but that death is not literal. Chris and his generation wanted change or death, and they had impossible expectations for drugs. Drugs provide only an illusion of change; in actual fact they encourage passivity and not changing. They make it seem as though everything were done, when in reality everything remains to be done.

The Dark Mother

For Chris, drugs opened the door to the magic of the moment and distracted him from his maniacal self-awareness. Unfortunately, they also became a dark mother who was slowly devouring him. He wanted the Dionysian esctasy never to end; he wanted to go on nursing on the psychedelic baby formula forever. Drugs increased his vitality, made him feel all powerful, and led him into a world of magic. A few years later, though, Chris found himself trapped in a life that seemed endlessly dreary and dull. Drugs, which had kept him flying so high for so long, were now dragging him down into the pits.

Although drugs had provided meaningful initiations for several of his friends, for Chris they led to a life of sickness and crime. When he finally got fed up with living like a criminal in order to pay for his daily dose of cocaine, he decided to seek help for his drug addiction; then, the following year, he plunged into the depths of alcoholism. The figure of Dionysus drowned in a barrel of wine represents Chris perfectly at this time in his life. At the age of thirty, Chris had become a favorite son of Dionysus.

A Psychological Profile of Chris

By the time he started his second detoxification program, Chris was no longer a typical baby boomer—he did fit the typical image of the alcoholic, though. He required constant oral gratification; he needed to be nourished and attended. He turned every conversation to himself and his own experiences; he insisted on being the center of attention. He also had strong aggressive impulses, and he would go to any lengths to avoid the distress he felt when he was alone.[16]

In his everyday life Chris would become enraged if his need for attention was not satisfied, and he would try to drown his disappointment and hostility by drinking. For Chris, alcohol served as a substitute for affection. He drank as a way of hurting the people around him, too, when he believed that they hadn't shown enough care and concern for him. He never realized that his attitudes were forms of self-punishment that led to masochistic degradation. He did not feel excessively guilty about his outbursts of aggression, although he did fear the rejections of his wife and friends.

Chris needed to drink continually in order to gain a sense

---

16. These typical characteristics of the alcoholic are taken from a study by E. Fromm and M. Maccoby, *Social Character in a Mexican Village* (Englewood Cliffs, N.J.: Prentice Hall, 1970), chap. 8, pp. 156–178.

of power and well-being. He wanted to be completely independent of others, especially of women, and he tried to hide any appearance of vulnerability or sensitivity in him. He believed that women found him irresistible, and he was always ready to defend his honor, by force if necessary. In the final analysis, Chris the long-haired freak had turned into Chris the macho man.

Macho behavior indicates an attitude of male superiority. It expresses men's desire to wield power over women and to keep them in subservient positions. The macho attitude is more revealing of a fear of women, though, than of any real conviction of superiority. Macho behavior lets a man compensate for his feelings of weakness, dependency, and passivity; the apparent toughness of macho behavior is only a facade. Like Chris, many men nevertheless still tend to adopt macho attitudes. They do not really feel like men unless they follow the macho model. Fortunately, though, the idea that real men don't cry is going out of fashion.

Mommy and Daddy Alcoholics

Chris is what can be called a "matriarchal" alcoholic: he has succumbed to his mother's power. He lives in a world that is dominated by women, and he is more dependent on them than he is on other men. The matriarchal alcoholic often comes from a single-parent family in which the mother never knew the father. She is both permissive and sadistic with her son, overprotective, and intolerant of his attempts to be independent. She thinks she is protecting him from the outside world, when in fact she is breaking down his initiative and his confidence in himself.

The "patriarchal" alcoholic differs from Chris. This alcoholic attempts to live in harmony with the patriarchal ideal. Unfortunately, he is too passive and dependent to stand up to a woman, and he is an automatic loser in the war of the sexes. Often he marries a woman who is dominating and destructive. Since he cannot find the strength to stand up to her, he takes refuge in alcohol, he escapes from the home and tries to rediscover his enjoyment of life. Only when he is drunk has he the courage to confront his wife; then he beats her. The patriarchal alcoholic shares with Chris a weakness with regard to women, and an independence and virility that have been replaced by a sadistic aggressivity.

When the Model Breaks Down

Anthropologists who have studied alcoholism at the social level conclude that whenever the structure of a society is clearly defined—clearly matriarchal or clearly patriarchal—there are relatively few alcoholics. In matriarchal societies men do not have constantly to prove their manhood or struggle for power that is not theirs anyway. In patriarchal societies, men's authority is not called into question. In Western patriarchal societies, however, the traditional power of men is eroding; as the statistics show, this erosion coincides with an increase in the incidence of alcohol abuse.[17]

The breakdown of the patriarchal model is particularly pronounced where I live in Quebec, which suffered conquest by the British. Wherever a people has been conquered—the Mexican Indians by the Spanish, the native peoples of Canada and the United States by the French and English—one of the classic responses to a society's loss of power is alcoholism.

In considering the story of Chris, it is necessary to understand that living in a single-parent family without a father may predispose the children to substance abuse: the father is simply not there to block the route to his sons' symbiotic dependency.

---

17. The 1980 statistics regarding alcohol consumption in various countries are as follows: France tops the list with an average per capita consumption of 14.8 liters of 100% alcohol per year; Canada is in the 16th position with 9.1 liters per capita; and the United States is in 19th place with 8.7 liters per capita. Four times more men than women are alcoholics; single people, divorcees, and the unemployed drink more than other population groups. (Source: *Alcohol in Canada, a National Perspective*, 2nd revised edition. Ottawa: Health and Welfare Canada, 1984).

In consequence, the son never learns to resist his oral cravings or his aggressive impulses. It is essential for all fathers to become aware of these realities and to assume their responsibilities toward their children, particularly after a divorce.

Chris is a perfect example of addiction and of imprisonment in the maternal world. He suffers extremely with what all lost sons carry around deep inside them. It is no coincidence that Dionysus is not only the god of drink, but also the god of masks and of the theater—where individual characteristics are magnified into caricatures. What is latent in others is blatant in Chris. Here is the most dramatic incidence of the breakdown of masculine identity caused by the father's absence. Will we sons find Spirit at the bottom of the wine barrel? Will we continue on our road to initiation and rediscover virility that is mature and not fearful of women?

THE DIRECTOR'S EPILOGUE

Well, folks, that's the end of our show. It's time to say goodbye to all these sons who are looking for their fathers and trying, sometimes desperately, to break out of their dominant mother complexes. In the past few weeks of working with these actors, I have developed a lot of affection for them. As I keep telling them, they don't have to stop acting like this or like that, but they should start questioning their obsessive behaviors and their unthinking identifications with the characters they play. For each of them, the challenge is to break away from the script and to become a real man.

You may be wondering, "What would happen if the hero were no longer dominated by his mother complex? Would the theater have to close down for lack of actors? When the actors all become "men," who then will perform for us? Who will be left to lead our heavy hearts down into the realm of death? If the seducers and eternal adolescents all succumb to an excessive dose of responsibility, who will be left to tempt us into doing or thinking what we don't want to do or think? What a catastrophe it would be if all the drunks became sober and all the good boys stopped being nice!"

Have no fear. Even if psychoanalysis manages to release all these characters from their strange forms of imprisonment—which would take a very long time indeed at the rate things are going—the theater would not have to shut down. The heroes will always be heroes, and the seducers will always be seducers. Since the actors will no longer be ruled by their characters, however, and since they will be free now to live their own lives, they will be able to play their roles—when they choose to play them—with a lot more vigor and vitality. The heroes will be all the more courageous, and their brilliant exploits will win even greater applause. The seducers will go on charming us, and the homosexuals will continue making us ask questions. Granted, the drunks will no doubt drink less, and there will be fewer suicides; the celebration will be all the more joyous. Everyone will still wear his mask, but no one will be enslaved by it.

THREE

The Fear of Intimacy

SEXUAL INTIMACY

As was explained in the first chapter, the father's absence may lead to the son's fear of the woman's body. When a man has become separated from his mother, his feelings of ambiguity toward his partners express his profound fear of intimacy. Allan, Michael, Fred, and the others are all frightened of getting involved in deep, intimate relationships. They are unable to stay in touch with themselves when they become involved with others—with sexual partners especially. In bed, as on stage, they cannot avoid playing their roles.

Intimacy

How can we speak of intimacy? How can we talk about it in a way that makes us more intimate with ourselves?

The *Oxford English Dictionary* defines *intimacy* as "close familiarity." The word *intimate* is derived from the Latin *intimus,* which means *innermost*. Intimacy is further defined as the "state of being personally intimate."[1] The term has conno-

---

1. *The Compact Edition of the Oxford English Dictionary,* vol. 1. Oxford University Press, 1976, p. 1470.

tations of familiarity, friendship, privacy, comfort, and close connection. Its opposites are externality, superficiality, coldness, and formality.

Whether we desire it or fear it, intimacy intimidates us. One of the many paradoxes of inner depth, of intimacy, is we miss it when we don't have it and yet it can become intolerable when we do have it.

Caresses That Burn

Bert is a fifty-five-year-old industrialist; he's a pleasant, cultivated man, somewhat avant-garde in certain aspects of his personality. His father was a wealthy alcoholic who lived only at night. His father did his best to crush all initiative in his son, so that Bert developed a negative father complex. He lost confidence in himself and mistrusted the people he worked with. He is still haunted by the father who rejected him, and every time he has a glass of wine he sees the image of a drunken man vomiting on a restaurant floor. He finds himself attracted to this man, although he does not want to become an alcoholic himself. The harmful influence of the inner father is still at work.

Bert's relationship with his mother was not much better. She was a cold, authoritarian woman, who was feared by the employees in the family business. She did manage to instill moral values in her son. On the inside, Bert is still a prisoner of the conflict that caused so much trouble in his early family life: he doesn't know whether to obey his father or his mother. When he is under the influence of the mother complex, he feels cold and rigid, subject to the mockery of his inner father; when he has a drink or makes love, he feels guilty about letting himself go.

Bert has been divorced for more than ten years. He lives alone in a huge house in the country. He is frightened of women. One night after making love, he dreamed that his mother had grown wings and was flying in circles above his bed. The morning after, like most mornings after, he felt so much guilt that for several hours he had thoughts of committing suicide.

This episode reminds me of the Greek myth of Cybele and Attis.[2] The goddess Cybele is at once mother, wife, and lover of the extremely handsome Attis. When she realizes that Attis is cheating on her with a young nymph, in a fit of anger she makes him insane. Attis, in his madness, castrates himself. Bert's mother fits the primitive stereotype of Cybele, a vicious woman who poisons her son's relations with the opposite sex. It is no wonder Bert has trouble with erections, since in a sense he has been castrated. His masculinity and his ability to penetrate are blocked by his never having separated himself from his mother, even though she has been dead for a long time.

Every time a mother gains such an imposing presence in a man's fantasy world, it is an indication that the time has come to cut the cord. Jung talks of the positive role of these witch images, which he views as unconscious compensations, indicating to the ego that the dependent relationship has gone on long enough. When psychological information like this can be acknowledged and used to bring about the necessary awareness, so much the better. In most cases, however, this compensation creates a distance between the man and the world of women. The inner work has not been done; the image of the witch-mother, "black and winged Cybele," is projected onto all women, especially onto their sexual parts, which become the abode of all manner of demons. This is why witches are often represented as repugnant nudes, as in Polanski's *Macbeth* or certain films by Fellini.

These images act on our reality. They condition our attitudes, inhibit our desires, and discourage us from any real, profound contact with the opposite sex. Whenever Bert feels negative emotions about his relationship with a woman, rather

2. Librairie Larousse, *New Larousse Encyclopedia of Mythology* (Halwyn, N.Y., 1959), p. 150.

than give vent to those feelings, he buys the woman flowers, takes her out to dinner, or treats her to a weekend in a fancy hotel. The more aggressive he feels toward her, the more he denies it in his outward behavior. The value of his presents seems directly proportional to the intensity of his negative feelings. It is hardly surprising that his companion is unable to satisfy his needs, since he himself refuses to recognize them. He lives in terror, frightened of being devoured. Every woman becomes an evil witch. He finds himself completely undermined by the repressed aggressiveness that paralyzes him and prevents him from getting an erection.

Men have less trouble admitting to problems of sexual impotence than they do acknowledging the feelings of rage and vulnerability that lie behind this impotence. They see the problem as strictly sexual. Clearly, few men would feel up to the task of making love to the great mother goddess who has the power to grant life and to take it away. The fear of being gobbled up in one bite does not exactly create a conducive climate for the act of love.

The first dream Bert worked on in therapy was this: he was on an island and kept hiding in a hole in the earth because he was frightened of the inhabitants on the other side of the island: primitive, dangerous men who killed everybody they met. This image shows us a different truth about Bert's psychological state: in his dream, the inhabitants of the other side of the island are not evil witches, they are men. Could it be that Bert fears his own violence, the very violence he would need to use to sever the original link binding his ego to the mother complex?

Bert's fear of women's sexual parts is one problem, but behind his impotence and masked aggression is another fear: the fear of being touched. A woman's caresses and physical affection have a devastating effect on him: each time he is touched he feels as if he is being burned. Caresses hurt him because they open old wounds deep inside him, wounds that resulted from his intense, unfulfilled desire for affection. Bert prefers to leave his desire dormant rather than to risk, yet again, the possibility of rejection and loss. Intimacy wounds him because it is beyond his control; he is torn between wanting to run away and letting himself wallow in affection. He is frightened of turning into a child again, a child at the mercy of the hungry dragon.

Bert has finally managed to overcome his obsessive anxieties and to establish a relationship with an adequate partner. I use the word "adequate" because one of his strategies was to make love only with women whom he in no way desired. This helped him keep his anxieties down to a tolerable level. Bert's new companion has reawakened his strong desire for fusion with another, the desire he had kept in check by living an austere, solitary life. In rediscovering his need for others, however, Bert has also discovered a possessiveness that surprises him. He becomes mad with jealousy at the thought that someone else might make advances to his girlfriend. This new obsession indicates the full extent of his internal insecurity. He doesn't approve of this attitude of his and tries to overcome his anxieties, but all to no avail: the anxieties are stronger than he is.

When an individual cannot "have" his parents enough, this often results in his being wounded by intimacy. Intimacy is what he wants, what he cries out for with his whole heart, but it is also what he fears the most. Bert is frightened of the cold but doesn't want to go into a warm house. Men like him, who did not receive adequate parenting, need to keep themselves at a certain distance from others. They may seem cool and collected on the outside, but most of the time there is despair and existential anguish behind the confident, superior attitudes of these men who seem on top of it all.

Running Short of Women

In his film *Casanova,* Fellini creates a living fresco of men's most primitive fantasies. Like a lot of men today, Casanova can make love to many women without touching or being touched by them in an emotional sense. He is incapable of feeling emotions for them because emotions *bind* one person to another, and these bonds for him would be the kiss of death. The moment he lets himself love, Casanova dies, as it were. Therefore he protects himself against the emotions of love and devotes himself to further conquests.[3]

To feel like a man, Casanova constantly needs a mirror in which to view his virility. Consequently, he is frightened of running short of women. When a man thinks he is running short of women, he surely needs reassurance about his own sexual identity.

Here is the example of Arnold, a man in his early thirties. Arnold is not a Don Juan, but his case does shed light on the dynamics involved in the need for a female mirror.

Arnold went through a very difficult period after his girl-friend's father died, because for several months she lost all interest in lovemaking. He then started having frequent homosexual fantasies, which made him ashamed because he no longer felt like a man. His fantasies were focused on the person of a physiotherapist, a middle-aged man with a hairy chest and an imposing build. During the same period, this man was treating Arnold for injuries to his arm. That a "father" could take care of him and be capable of gentleness was a complete revelation for Arnold. His own father, handicapped and alcoholic, had imposed a military discipline on the household and had regularly beaten his sons. In reaction to this treatment, Arnold had identified with his devout, silent mother, who submitted to her husband out of a sense of duty. In his adult life, Arnold retained the masochistic attitudes of his mother, and in his fantasies he dreamed of his father taking him

---

3. Various critics have contested Fellini's interpretations of the confessions of Casanova, claiming the filmmaker has confused him with Don Juan. In actual fact Casanova maintained long relationships with his mistresses by letter, and he had deep feelings for them. Compare the detached cynicism of Don Juan.

roughly in order to get the pleasure his wife, Arnold's mother, did not provide him. In the period during which he could not obtain a reflection of his own virility by making love with his girlfriend, Arnold developed homosexual fantasies. He also dressed in women's clothes and masturbated while looking in a mirror.

Arnold's abusive father had sown the seeds of doubt in him about his sexual identity. His homosexual fantasizing and his cross-dressing were symbolic expressions of his desire to seduce his father and absorb his strength. In certain tribes a homosexual relationship with an older man is an integral part of the initiation ritual for adolescent boys. In other cultures, the son must drink the father's sperm in order to gain his own potential for virility. The Greeks elevated pederasty to the rank of an institution. Most men today, especially those who had missing fathers, have latent homosexual fantasies; their need for a father's recognition has become contaminated by their sexual needs.

For men, then, the lack of a father's confirmation of their status as a male creates an insecurity about their sexual identity. This insecurity drives them to search continually for mirrors of their virility in the eyes of women. When a man says he's running short of women, he might just as well say he's running short of men.

Pinup Girls

Let's go back to the perennial question of desire. In our childhood, sex seemed the deadliest of sins, desire was denied, and repression reigned. In consequence, some of us relegated sexuality to the shadowy realms of pornography and sex shops.

Men turn to pornography to find the missing mirrors of their virility. The women in the magazines a man leafs through call to him, desire him, whisper to him about his big penis. They reflect a strong, powerful image of himself. With his paper women, a man takes refuge in rituals of masturbation that are actually rituals of narcissistic reequilibration that reestablish his self-love. Compulsive masturbation, in fact, is very often linked to feeling deprived of affection. In their rites for the goddess Kali, priests, who are not allowed to have heterosexual relations, masturbate as they dance before the effigies of the mother goddess.

These forms of behavior are related to the fantasy of the motherly prostitute who is filled with understanding and acceptance, and ready to satisfy a man's every need and desire. Many a man dreams of sinking into the arms of a pretty, gentle geisha and being transported to rapturous realms of delight. The powerful fantasies that dominate the worlds of pornography and prostitution blind us to the tragic and sordid social realities on which they are based.

Women often reject pornography; they are offended, quite justifiably, by the exploitation of women that pornography reflects. But in terms of his fantasies, the consumer of porn is not simply an exploiter of the female body. "A man running short of women" identifies with women just as much as with men: he penetrates and is penetrated. Not only does he find satisfaction for his homosexual fantasies in pornography, he also finds in it the symbiosis, the feeling of joining with another that is part of all love relationships. These are feelings he either cannot—or will not—allow himself in his real relationships.

A remark I heard on a radio talk show, "Pornography is eroticism with the lights on,"[4] describes it perfectly: it is a vision of sex that is crude, direct, and masculine, a vision that men find difficult to share with women because they think they are too delicate. Men must show great maturity in accepting their own need for raw virility in their sexual relations; most of the time they lose their animal spontaneity as soon as they take off their pants. Then they must rely solely on their technical prowess. That spontaneity, however, is the very foundation of the erotic energy that women seek in men. Real

4. Pierre Bourgeault, *Plaisir*, CBF 690, March, 1988.

sharing is born when a man lets himself become more daring, when he lets himself feel good. Unfortunately, men only let themselves really feel good when they are alone with a magazine or a porno film. The adoration they show for women then exceeds their flesh-and-blood partners' wildest expectations.

Can we really help men and women understand what is involved in their sexual relations by condemning pornography? I have very real doubts about this. Condemning pornography only reinforces the guilt men already feel; it drives them even further away from real women, whom they can observe finally only through a little hole at a peep show. Voyeurism is a most striking expression of fear of intimacy: it is having sex from a distance, in hiding. It's hard to know whether to laugh or to cry at it. Only by penetrating to the core of pornographic reality and fully exploring the realities of its underlying fantasies can we hope to understand it—and perhaps change it.

Like women who read Harlequin romances, men who use pornography are creating a distance between themselves and the reality of the opposite sex. Porn is a fantasy culture, and it has its place, so long as it doesn't usurp reality. Some men dream of geishas and some women dream of white knights. Meanwhile our love stories are battlefields on which we wage our insidious struggles for power, as if one side must succumb to the fantasies of the other. We find ourselves in a deadlock: pornography proliferates; women grow angrier; and men are ruled by impotence.

Inflatable Dolls, Disposable Women

One day a friend confided to me that he was head over heels in love with a woman who smoked and drank too much. He loved having sex with her; it made him more open and relaxed, but the idea of a long-term relationship set off in him an obsessive need to reform his companion and the bags under her eyes and her chewed fingernails. She just "had" to stop poisoning herself with coffee, alcohol, and cigarettes. *Her* addictions were making *him* sick.

We are all prisoners of the myth of the inflatable doll: the sex doll that can be blown up, used, deflated, repaired, stored away, or replaced. This doll is the culmination of our throw-away civilization. We do not want to see on our lovers' bodies the marks of their lives or the marks of their pregnancies. We want our mirrors forever perfect and unblemished—so they will hide our own flaws as well. We expect women to be ideal and reparable, yet we expect them to accept our flabbiness, our acne scars, our sloppy clothes, scruffy beards, body odor, bald heads, and so on.

We not only drain women of their reality, we also drain life itself of its reality, out of life with all its scars and ravages. Brave eternal sons that we are, we even drain away the idea of physical death. We have become frighteningly adept at ignoring the signs of the destruction of our natural environment. Only recently have we discovered, with alarm, the realities of acid lakes, polluted rivers, and toxic air. Each person bears the marks of his physical, emotional, and spiritual evolution; everything that exists in the world bears the marks of its own history. To live outside that reality leads directly to self-destruction. In bed, when we suddenly discover our partner's wrinkles, the discovery seems so intolerable that we immediately set about looking for a partner who is younger and less marked by living.

I wonder whether my friend who loved the addict would get as much sustenance from their sexual relations if his partner did not have problems of substance dependency? Of course it's not always simple, and the heart has reasons unknown to reason, but clearly we are indeed constantly cutting things away from our lovers' realities. Then we find ourselves complaining that something is missing. It's true: something *is* missing. Our presence in the physical reality of the world, in its rich and intricate beauty, is missing.

The Cult of Venus

"How can I channel my sexuality?" André asked me late one afternoon. He was exhausted, and I too was tired, having reached the last of a long week of appointments. The light streaming into the office was warm and comfortable, though; it was one of those winter evenings when the sun goes down too early; one feels happy just being inside on such an evening. My therapeutic relationship with André was comfortable too. We had known each other for several years, and although he had completed his therapy, we went on seeing each other once a month, just to keep in touch.

He felt he was masturbating too much when he wasn't in contact with his girlfriend; their relationship seemed troubled, and he desired her only for sex. He felt a great deal of guilt about all this, and he talked about his sexual activities in a deprecating manner, as simply "getting his rocks off."

I drew his attention to the terms with which he expressed himself. Did he not feel a certain pleasure in "getting his rocks off?" Was there not something in the act of greater value than the simple physical release of tension? "Of course," he replied; there were his own fantasies, and there were also his girlfriend's gentleness and affection. So why was he talking about their sex in such a derogatory way, and why did he feel so guilty?

I told him the story of Venus, the ancient goddess of love and beauty. André's choice of words degraded Venus; he did not pay her her due. Was he not treating her like a minor goddess, a prostitute in the shadowy corners of his psyche? A greater appreciation for Venus might enable André to set aside his guilt and express to his partner how grateful he is for the hours of warmth and erotic pleasure he spends in her company. His girlfriend might meet his frankness with disapproval, but his frankness would at least let André put an end to the division within himself.

Why can't all erotic relationships be celebrations of Venus?[5]

---

5. A recent book by Benoîte Groulx, *Les Vaisseaux du coeur* (Vessels of the

Why are erotic relationships always enacted in silence or guilt? Is it not possible for us to own our desire and our sexuality? Why is there so much discomfort connected with such a vital force as erotic love? Why do we have so much trouble recognizing love as a divinity, as a distinct psychological force? Can sex never be more than simply "getting one's rocks off?"

Freud stated that sex, or Eros, is the force that connects us to the world and obliges us to get out of our own selves. Why do we not honor and celebrate Eros with poetry? Is our civilization so poor that our cult of Venus must be reduced to an obsession with pornography? There are other societies in which sex is accepted as noble and admirable. The Kama Sutra cultivates the art of erotic positions as bridges between mortals and God. Indian temples display explicit images of the union of gods and goddesses. Erotic Japanese prints testify that sexual acts are highly regarded in that particular culture. Even in the Bible, the Song of Solomon does not exactly beat around the bush in its celebration of human love.

When we deny a temple to Venus, we become victims of the literal aspect of sex. Sex becomes a "piece of ass," devoid of the exaltation of the soul in contact with beauty. Mohammed himself claimed that the best time for prayer is immediately after making love, when the heart is completely open to the divinity.

The Greeks believed that if a person suffered from a sexual obsession, he should not appeal to Apollo, but rather to Venus for greater self-discipline. Illnesses were thought to stem from the individual's lack of respect for a particular divinity. Seen from this perspective, a sexual obsession would indicate not an overrating of this natural force, but rather an undervaluing of it. When powerful forces are scorned and repressed they go underground, and then from the depths of the unconscious they exert irresistible pressures on the conscious self. The road

---

Heart), tells of precisely this kind of erotic passion between a man and a woman of different social classes, that lasts for more than forty years.

to sexual healing begins with a profound acceptance of our sexual being, not with its repression or with futile attempts to control it.

We must emphasize rather than diminish the importance of sexuality in order to understand it. To reject Venus is to sever our capacity to relate to the world and its incredible beauty. Conversely, embracing sexuality allows us to develop in erotic relationship with the whole universe; it opens up our senses and our sensuality. It is not self-eroticism, but a process of revitalization; it fosters our desires to share ourselves intimately with others.

A society that does not celebrate sex and beauty, and which refuses to recognize their divinity, is clearly condemning itself to the scourge of pornography. Pornography is the insidious revenge of an offended goddess. She demands that we seek intimacy with her.

Venus calls into question our society's troubles with sexual intimacy. Our society is not yet ready to consider sexuality as one of its distinct components, probably because of the freedom this might imply. Authentic, intimate sexuality remains unrecognized in all our formal structures, from the church to the couple in love.

"Sex plays an extraordinarily important part in our lives because it is perhaps the only deep, firsthand experience we have. Intellectually and emotionally we conform, imitate, follow, obey. There is pain and strife in all our relationships, except in the act of sex. This act, being so different and beautiful, we become addicted to, so it in turn becomes a bondage."[6]

Emotional Incest Between Mothers and Sons

In one of his public lectures, the psychoanalyst Julien Bigras mentioned that a carefully documented study of more than a

---

6. J. Krishnamurti, *The Second Krishnamurti Reader* (Penguin Books, 1973), p. 239.

hundred families in the United States revealed no cases of incest in families in which there was a high level of physical closeness between parents and young children. It is becoming increasingly acceptable for a father to take a bath with his three- or four-year-old daughter or son; that is as it should be. This kind of behavior is a good way to prevent incest since the child's need for affection and his natural curiosity are gratified by physical contact.

If there is no contact between parent and child, these unsatisfied needs are relegated to areas of sexuality. The sexual act becomes overly charged, and all forms of touching become suspicious. It's a vicious circle: the more we need affection, the more sexual desire we feel, since it's the only way we know of getting affection. Sexuality has been liberated, but we still have to liberate touching, holding, and all the other forms of physical affection between women, between men, between women and men, and between parents and children. We have to create a world that is less sexually divided, one in which gentleness, sensuousness, and the shared pleasure of mutual desire are all accepted and welcomed.

A friend told me about a dream of his. The dream highlights a reality that is often obscured by the preoccupation with incest between fathers and daughters: the phenomenon of emotional incest between mothers and sons. My friend titled his dream "The Black World."

I find I am looking down on the backyard of my childhood family home. I awake in a world that is completely smooth, like a theater stage covered with plastic gym mats. Everything is black, without roughness, and bathed in a soft dim light. It is very comfortable and velvety. At the very center of this stage lies a woman I know. She is dressed in white and her unbuttoned blouse reveals her ample breasts. She wants to make love. I approach and lie half on top of her, but I sense a presence behind me. I turn around. My mother is standing in a doorway, dressed in white. She is wearing a very tight-fitting wool dress slit up the sides, like a prostitute's. My mother, a heavyset woman with large breasts, is radiant. She talks to me in a voice urgent with passion. She is happy to see me, her son, and she sings me a song of love: "Oh my son! How happy I am to see you! How I desire you! How I desire your ass and your balls and your penis! How I desire you, my son!" She invites me to make love. I look at her in the doorway, and I am frightened. I am deeply shaken by the intense desire she feels for me. At that moment I understand that what has always frightened me about women is precisely this power symbolized by the strength of my mother's desire for me.

This dream had a tremendously liberating effect on my friend; it revealed the whole unconscious side of his relationship with his mother. All his life he had sensed her longing and desire for him, without ever being clearly aware of it. How much easier it would have been for him if he had learned as a teenager that he wasn't the only one to experience desire, that women experience it too. Knowing this would have obviated much of the clumsiness and guilt in his later relations with women. The more the carnal aspect of love is ignored in the family context, the more it is likely to provoke excessive fear and curiosity in sons. Desire that is unacknowledged and unconscious becomes destructive and omnivorous.

Although the existence of the body must be acknowledged in the family, it goes without saying that parents must restrain their own desires. Once their sons or daughters have reached puberty, parents must respect the incest barrier and avoid ambiguous physical gestures. Otherwise they force their children to erect the barrier themselves. A child in this position is likely to build a very strong protective shell around himself; this shell will not only protect him, though: it will also isolate him and prevent him from feeling his own desires. He will feel guilty about his urges and try to repress them so as not to excite his father or mother—which would lead to his losing his physical integrity.

The Fellini film *Casanova* has a scene in which some men have to make love with an enormously fat woman who has fire in her vagina. The fire represents women's awakened desire, which in the final analysis is the very thing that frightens men most.

I think here of the example of Elaine, who for months put up with her partner complaining about her lack of sexual desire. Yet to her amazement, when she wanted to make love two nights in a row, he moved to the living-room sofa, claiming he'd had too much stress at work that day! When she's the one who exhibits desire, he prefers to mow the lawn or do odd jobs around the house.

Man has always been fascinated by the female body. The reason is simple: the woman's sexual parts are where he came from. All the fears I've discussed here, all the avoidances and strategies men use to keep women at a distance, are finally comprehensible: she who gave us life may also be capable of taking it from us.

THE INTIMATE COUPLE

The Myth of Intimacy

Jan Bauer, a Jungian analyst, believes intimacy should be looked at from a new angle, because real intimacy between the sexes is a rather recent phenomenon. There's certainly no lack of evidence for her contention. Intimacy, in fact, is an entirely modern requirement imposed on couples. Until the last century, marriages were often arranged by the family. Even in our parents' generation, couples who married for love often stayed together only out of a sense of duty. They performed their functions and their roles often to the detriment of their personal happiness. Also, there has often been a strict division of the sexes in the areas of sport, education, and religion. Our contemporary insistence on intimacy now exacerbates old fears and creates new expectations. We should remember that in all the great romantic myths, like Romeo and Juliet or Tristan and Isolde, the heroes die young; clearly this can be seen as a medieval commentary on the chances for the survival of intimate love relationships.

Intimacy between people of the same sex is not exactly common either. Among women, who are more in touch with their inner feelings than are men, there is perhaps a greater level of sharing. When men come together, though, they do things together, or they talk about what they've accomplished, but they almost never express their feelings. Even between really close friends there are still strong taboos discouraging intimacy.

Basically, there is no intimacy between the sexes or among people of the same sex today because most people do not have an intimacy with themselves—they have no living relationship with what is going on inside them.

The Language of Love

On the subject of intimacy between the sexes, Annie Leclerc provides a beautifully phrased reminder: "The language of Eros does not establish enmity between the sexes, but rather an awareness of their differences."[7] She shows how sexual differences take their meaning from the language of love, the language that is outside the sharing of power between men and women. "To every man, Eros dictates his destiny as a man: you must win the love of a woman. To every woman, Eros dictates her destiny as a woman: you must nurture love in your heart, and preserve it. Neither men nor women invented this. Eros did. Eros, their shared religion."[8]

Annie Leclerc interprets a man's need for achievement and mastery not as a wish to exploit women, but rather as an urge toward making himself loved by a woman. Leclerc does not

---

7. Annie Leclerc, *Hommes et femmes* (Men and Women), (Paris: Grasset, coll. Le Livre de poche, no. 6150, 1985), p. 69.

8. Ibid, p. 39.

advocate new powers for women, although she recognizes that these are necessary; rather she seeks to return to women the power they have always had: their power to love.

This is a refreshing concept, to which I would add the following thoughts: as long as we remain caught up in the language of power, the difference between the sexes is intolerable; it is founded on the injustices men impose on women. For men, power has been the ultimate goal, throughout human history, but human history itself began in complementarity between men and women. We men have held Eros in contempt, disregarding the intimacy of love and our own need for it; we have forgotten that all our goals lose meaning when our desires are not directed toward the love of another person.

Viewed from this angle, women's present access to contraception is a fundamental and irreversible development in our history. The availability of contraception today signals an end to men's abuse of women's reproductive functioning, for the greater good of us all. It allows humanity, for the first time, to explore the reality beneath the traditional dictates of a division of the sexes. Women can now demonstrate that men do not have a monopoly on the external world. And men now must show that they are not helpless in areas traditionally assigned to women, that they too are capable of feelings, domestic skills, and interiority.

It would be a mistake, however, to take this new sharing of power as a harbinger of a unisex future for the human race. The language of love gives life with its fullness; life itself is made possible by sexual difference. This difference need not suggest inequality; rather it motivates our search for sharing. "Eros always speaks the same language, a language we all understand. Love is the ultimate good for everyone, and it can only come about fully when it is fully reciprocal."[9]

The following example provides a good illustration of the problems that can arise for a modern couple when sexual

9. Ibid., p. 63.

differences between men and women automatically give rise to the exploitation of one sex by the other.

Eva has come to see me for the first time in several months. Since our last meeting she has put an end to a relationship that had been making her miserable, and she has become involved with a man ten years older than she; he loves her and she loves him. She has come to consult me because she is two months pregnant and is not sure she wants to have the child. Her argument goes like this:

The pregnancy means she will have to stop working for a certain time. It is very important for her to earn her own money, so that, as she puts it, her partner will not gain "power" in their relationship. She is frightened of becoming dependent on him; the very idea of it sends her into a tailspin.

The plot of Eva's tale thickened when she told her partner he was going to be a father. He went wild with joy; he was happy and proud, and in spite of his previous doubts, he agreed to get married. He suggested that Eva should stop working; he would earn all the money they needed himself over the next two years.

Instead of pleasing Eva, this idea mortifies her. Instead of welcoming it as a well-intentioned and generous offer, she regards it as a trap in which she has no intention of getting caught. She saw her own mother beaten and abused by a husband who was rarely at home. He controlled all the household finances and left his wife with complete responsibility for educating the children. Eva is unable to detach herself from this vision from the past. She believes that all men are potential exploiters.

Eva ended up having an abortion in her sixteenth week of pregnancy.

There was a striking image in one of Eva's dreams: a living bull crucified on the wall of a stable. No doubt this image prefigured her abortion, but it also symbolized her sacrifice of her own animal nature. So we see what happens when we think that different roles imply sexual inequality, which in turn implies male exploitation of women. To be fair to Eva, however, we must remember that it was reaction to her own family background that caused her to react so intensely to this situation.

When we view everything in terms of power, we do ourselves violence. We lose sight of that deep, natural impulse that transforms a man into a protector, hunter, and provider just at his very thought of becoming a father. This is the primitive reflex that has ensured the survival of our race. There may well be reasons to question this reflex, but how will we survive if we reject it and all our instinctive impulses? Our animal nature, forged through thousands of years of evolution, possesses its own wisdom, which cannot keep up with the speed of our recently acquired human reasoning. This wisdom now demands to be expressed in the language of Eros.

If Eva had been able to believe that she was not sacrificing her professional life for her husband, but rather for their relationship, she might have overcome her obsession with power. When a couple consciously envisions the fruit of their union to be a kind of "third partner," they can get beyond internal power struggles. Their attitude can render conflicts less subjective and create more room for agreement. The relationship can then become a mutual undertaking, which will require energy and sacrifice. The two are no longer at the service of one another, but at the service of the unity they share.

Letting Go

The basic problem with establishing intimacy seems to be the difficulty people have in letting themselves go and trusting one another. Intimacy involves abandoning oneself to another and staying in contact with oneself at the same time.

When engaged in sexual intimacy a man often wants to give pleasure to his partner or be given pleasure by her. He wants to act. To give or receive pleasure, though, he must *have* the pleasure himself: he must be present in it, inhabit it, and share it with his partner. When visiting the land of pleasure it is best to travel in pairs.

To avoid the dangers of impotence—sexual, physical, or emotional—men must accept the risk of getting in touch with their own desires and their own pleasure within the gaze of another. Letting go in this way gives rise to a sense of play between the two partners, a loving involvement in one another, a mutual companionship, and a shared intimacy.

Our differences can lead to the most appalling acts of violence and abuses of power, yet the same differences can also nurture love. The masculine and the feminine can simply be perceived as two different ways of viewing reality, an objectivity provided by nature that we do well to conform to. The nature of attraction and desire requires that I, man, must never be completely the same as you, woman; we must abolish our differences in love. We must lose and find ourselves in one another; in our deep continuity neither partner will be dominant or submissive; we will, at least for brief moments, experience the liberty and grace of being ourselves, together. At that point, joined by what is deepest in us, we will be freed of difference and forget where one of us begins and the other ends. At that point we will be finally intimate.

FOUR

Repressed Agression

IRON HANS

Lost sons are frightened of intimacy because they have lost touch with their inner strength, strength that is rooted in primitive energy and natural aggression. The father's presence provides the son access to this aggression. When the father is absent, the son cannot tap into his sex's inherent impulses. The son is subjected to his mother's restrictions; she is likely to be less tolerant of his instinctive aggressive behavior than his father might have been.

Maternal love often causes a mother to insist that her son be polite and reserved, never raise his voice, and never slam the door. This insistence is her way of holding on to him. Paradoxically, the mother's animus contrives to break her son's masculinity by means of violent actions and arguments. If the son's physical spontaneity is continually thwarted in this way, it gradually changes into hostility toward women and makes intimacy impossible.

A Contemporary Fable

One of the fairy tales collected by the Brothers Grimm provides a marvelous illustration of my ideas about aggressiveness.

Entitled "Iron Hans," it has been magnificently interpreted in the context of contemporary masculinity by the American poet Robert Bly.[1] Here is my summary of the story:

> The king's hunters were disappearing one by one whenever they ventured into a very distant part of the forest. No one could explain these disappearances. One day a young man came to the king's court in search of a job. He was told about the mysterious problem. The young hero then went off alone, with only his dog for company, to discover the truth about the disappearances.
>
> As he was walking past a pond, a hand emerged from the water, grabbed his dog, and dragged it down into the depths. The hunter felt terrible about losing his dog, so he had the king's servants empty the pond with buckets. At the very bottom they discovered a huge, wild, and primitive-looking man. His hair fell all the way down to his feet, and since it was rust colored, they called him "Iron Hans."
>
> The king rewarded the young hunter and had Iron Hans put into a cage, which was placed in the inner courtyard of the castle. Several days later, when the king's eight-year-old son was playing with his golden ball, it rolled right into the wild man's cage. Iron Hans of course refused to return the ball, but he made the boy an offer: if the child wanted his favorite toy back, he would have to give Hans the key to his cage.
>
> But where was this key? Iron Hans told the king's son that it was hidden under his mother's pillow. The boy waited until his parents had gone away for the day, and then he took the key. As soon as Iron Hans was free, he prepared to return to the forest. The boy, fearing he would be punished by his parents, begged Iron Hans to take him along. The wild man agreed to this, but warned him: "You will never see your

1. Bly, Robert, "What Men Really Want, a New Age Interview with Robert Bly by Keith Thompson," *New Age Journal*, May 1982, pp. 31–51.

*father and mother again!" Then he hoisted the lad onto his
shoulders, and the two of them disappeared into the woods.*

The Primitive Man Sleeps Under His Mother's Pillow

Iron Hans symbolizes the wild, primitive man who has been
repressed in the unconscious. This explains why he is found at
the bottom of a pond in a distant part of the forest. As with
Samson, his hair represents his vital, instinctive power, the
power associated with aggression, sex, and raw energy. There
is no room in the civilized life of the kingdom for this male
brute from the depths, so he is put in a cage.

The golden ball represents the nascent personality of the
king's son, potentially full and round. In order to develop
completely, the boy's personality must make contact with his
primitive energy. The golden ball rolls into Iron Hans' cage.

The story's most remarkable detail is the key to the cage
kept under the mother's pillow; this indicates that the son's
instinctive masculinity is controlled by the mother. This is
clearly what happens when the King his father can find no
better solution to his own identity problem than to put the
wild man in a cage.

Finally, when the young man runs away with Iron Hans, he
leaves the world of his family forever. Iron Hans will initiate
him into his vital, instinctive power so that the young man
will never again be a mommy's boy or a daddy's boy.

GETTING IT OUT

Pumping Adrenaline

A number of years ago I was struck by the singer Jacques Brel's
response to a journalist's question about how he spent his time
now that he was no longer singing. Brel's answer, delivered
with the utmost seriousness, was "I try to tire myself out." If
you watch young teenage boys playing among themselves, you
will be surprised at how aggressive their games are; they too

are trying to tire themselves out. Their parents are constantly amazed by the violence in the films their sons like watching. This aggressiveness is part of the rough-and-tumble way boys have of expressing affection; it also answers their need to get the adrenaline flowing, to get it out of their systems. In adult men this same need seems to explain their impulsiveness, their drive for self-affirmation, their quest for a challenge, for something to struggle for. By tiring themselves out with these drives and quests, men can find moments of peace and tranquility.

One of the things women have most trouble understanding about men is the pleasure they take in competing against one another: horsing around, provoking each other, playing rough. Women also have trouble understanding the violent need for "screwing" that comes over men, a need apparently not anchored in any rational context. Whether a challenge is physical or intellectual, men take a fierce pleasure in testing themselves. *They have to get it out!*

There is something aggressive in the male, something impulsive from which he cannot escape. "Aggressive" is used here in its nonpejorative sense; it describes a form of energy that expresses a sensible and appropriate self-affirmation. In this regard, aggressiveness is akin to sexual energy.

Does all this imply that men may secretly like war, since combat gives their lives an intensity they cannot find elsewhere? Women, for their part, find this intensity in conceiving and bearing children. For both men and women, nothing makes life more precious and more intense than running the risk of losing it.

A few years ago in a small city in the United States, I attended a parade of Vietnam War veterans. I was astounded when guys my own age started cheering wildly as soon as their regimental colors came into view. I wondered if they weren't actually making fun of the soldiers in the parade. My American friends assured me that the situation was quite the contrary: these men had loved the war.

In his book *Manhood*, the psychoanalyst Stephen Shapiro writes that in traditional male education, the emphasis placed on discipline, self-control, courage, and patriotism, is connected with the internal violence each man secretly holds within him. The man must learn to master this violence in order to use it in the service of his community.

Self-hatred and Scapegoats

When overly strict parents cannot tolerate their son's outbursts of anger or aggressiveness, the boy represses his brute impulses. Since he must release this energy in some way, he channels it in one or more of these directions:

1. *The aggression is turned inward and becomes self-hatred.* Self-loathing is expressed in an individual's constant guilt feelings, his pessimistic attitudes, the bitter sarcasm he directs against himself, and his compulsive unconscious behaviors (such as overeating, biting his fingernails, unreasonable cleanliness, or injuring himself). Self-hatred may also propel him into chronic depression.

2. *The repressed aggression finds a scapegoat.* Usually the individual chooses a person who is weaker than himself or who is from a social group he considers inferior (a person of color, for example, or a homosexual). Often the dominant parent actually selects the scapegoat; the son's prejudices are likely to be the same as his father's or mother's.

3. *The repressed aggression may be transformed into worship of the aggressor.* A tyrannical parent may be perceived as "wonderful" and his authority considered infallible. He becomes an object of admiration: "Daddy is always right." On the collective level, this devotion leads straight to fascism, a system in which the citizens believe that the dictator is beyond all criticism.

4. *The aggression becomes eroticized.* In this case two repressed impulses, sex and aggressiveness, become linked and they give rise to sadomasochistic fantasies and behavior. The sadist treats his partner in the same way his repressive parent

treated him, while the masochist adopts the attitudes of the parent who submitted to the other's domination. The adult masochist may also repeat his own submissive behavior.

Masculine Energy

I believe that a certain kind of forceful, penetrating, active energy is one of the foundations of masculine identity; a man who is out of touch with his impulses, or unable to control them, never feels himself to be a man. (I certainly don't mean to suggest that women are not dynamic or energetic, though.) A man must recognize himself in the god Phallos, with his erect penis; he must sense the particular kind of energy that makes him essentially different from women.

A man today sometimes finds himself trapped in this situation: the absence of his father has deprived him of contact with his own natural aggression and the ability to control it; consequently, he despises the masculine side of himself. The loss of these masculine values can be seen as a form of castration. It causes all sorts of internal difficulties.

What happens when a whole generation of men feel cut off from their aggressiveness? The problem does not disappear; it becomes unconscious. Iron Hans lives at the bottom of a pond in a distant forest. When repressed, men's inherent energy changes into hostility, inner rage, and sometimes violence. If it is misused or misdirected, the natural drive for self-affirmation will be constantly disrupting the individual's ability to function.

HOLDING BACK ANGER

A Paranoid Thug

Let us look at the example of Tony, an accountant in his thirties. At the beginning of my work with Tony, I was struck by his way of walking with his arms held a few inches from his body, as if he were always ready to protect himself. At the start of each session he would stare at me intensely with a sort of X-ray vision that I found vaguely disconcerting. What was he trying to reassure himself about?

Tony had grown up in a cold family environment. His father was a businessman, more concerned with his company than with his children. In early adolescence, Tony felt a great deal of aggression toward his father; he felt responsible for his father's heart attack. Tony's mother experienced totally unpredictable changes of mood: sometimes she was warm and attentive, often she was cold and indifferent. Tony learned to be constantly on his guard, ready for any eventuality.

Therapy with Tony went very slowly. For a long time he would simply tell me about the little things that had happened in his life, without any glimmer of emotion. From time to time he would ask whether our work would soon be finished. After several months of plodding along, he had the following dream:

> *I was in the corner grocery store, looking for something in one of the aisles. All of a sudden a man armed with a rifle burst into the store, intending to rob it. He looked nervous and wary, and he seemed rather paranoid. I thought I might be able to put him out of commission by hitting the back of his neck, but that would be risky for me. So I decided to play it safe and not do anything. Then the man standing beside me moved into action. The robber spun around and shot him. At this moment my girlfriend came into the store, completely unaware of what was happening. I wanted to protect her. I didn't want her to do anything to try to disarm the robber. I signaled to her to come over to me, and I lay down on top of her.*

When I asked what the robber made him think about, Tony depicted him as the worst sort of thug: he was not only nervous and paranoid, he was clearly a psychopath who could kill in cold blood without even blinking. Tony was proud of having saved his own skin by refusing to get involved. When I suggested that the robber might be a part of himself with which he had lost contact, he strongly denied this. Who wants to see himself as a psychopath? Tony argued that my interpretation didn't give enough credit to his own behavior in the dream: he had done what had to be done, and he had respected the rules of his superego![2] I explained that this was precisely the problem: once again he had done "what had to be done." He was so strongly "identified" with his superego that his spontaneity was completely smothered. I suggested that his refusal to attack the robber, to touch or confront him, might symbolize his way of avoiding contact with his own hostility. This avoidance cut him off from all the positive forces of his aggression. This was why the analysis was stagnating.

I explained to Tony that his unconscious way of handling his inner anger was to project it outward onto others. He was going through life always on his guard, carefully examining anyone he was involved with. The real paranoid, nervous character was himself, and the explosions of aggression that he feared were actually his own. I suggested that getting in touch with his repressed violence was the only way Tony could escape from the pattern of paranoid vigilance that was sapping his life energy.

I referred to the moment in his dream when he lay down on top of his girlfriend, protecting himself at the same time he was protecting her. He didn't want her to come into contact with his hostility or to trigger it by her actions in the dream— or in real life by her bothersome questions or intuitions. His situation with his girlfriend was problematic. For two years now Tony had kept her dangling, willing neither to live with her nor to put an end to their relationship. I proposed that he

---

2. The mother's influence is only one element in the superego, which is composed of all the social and moral restrictions that have accumulated from the individual's relationship with his parents, his religion, and his education. It may overwhelm or stifle him when it inhibits all his impulsive desires that don't conform with its dictates.

accept the dream psychopath as a way of finding the courage to kill the relationship or to overcome his hesitations and enter into it fully.

A Soft-skinned Tiger

Roger provides us with yet another example of holding back anger. Retired and in his sixties, he had had a very successful career as a businessman. He was a pleasant fellow, who would readily break into a smile. One revealing detail about him immediately caught my attention: his way of shaking hands. He would hold his hand out as a sign of greeting, but he never actually closed it over my hand. It was a noncommittal gesture in which he didn't give anything of himself. Once he became aware of it, however, he made a point of shaking hands in a friendlier manner.

Roger's father was extremely demanding and authoritarian; he had considered Roger a good-for-nothing. The father was a real tyrant, with his children and with his submissive, depressive wife. Roger's mother left him behind her in a store once, having simply forgotten that she had taken him shopping with her. As a means of surviving and forestalling abandonment, Roger had grown an affable, smiling shell around himself. He started therapy for a problem of sexual impotence. The following is one of the first dreams he told me about:

> I was at a cabin in the woods, discussing with my colleague what we should do to defend ourselves against a tiger that had been skulking around the area. My colleague decided to go out and locate the tiger. Meanwhile I decided to get a pitchfork from the basement; I was convinced I could keep the tiger at bay with a pitchfork. I glanced out the window and saw my dog standing completely motionless, transfixed by something he saw. It was the tiger, much larger than we had thought, well fed, and seemingly soft to the touch. He was moving toward the cabin. I wondered what on earth I should do.

For the dreamer, the softness of the tiger's skin recalled the soft skin of his wife. I explained to Roger as I had to Tony that he was probably trying to defend himself against his own ferocity, against the tiger within himself. He projected this onto his wife, whose negative judgments he feared. The motionless dog suggested his impotence problems. I connected these problems with Roger's ferocious, hostile feelings about his wife. He was frightened of being devoured by her, but in reality he feared being attacked by his own inner violence.

Tony's and Roger's dreams share a common element: the two dreamers are frightened of being killed as a result of contacting the aggressive parts of themselves. Their fear, in a sense, is quite legitimate, since they indeed cannot emerge unscathed from contact with their repressed hostilities. This brings up an important psychological fact: the structure of the ego is changed by its relations with unconscious dimensions of the self. If we recognize and accept the murderer or the enraged beast within ourselves, the deep emotional experience of this recognition will modify our conscious attitudes; as individuals we will change. The sad truth is that, though we advocate change, we actually fight against it with all our strength since it often appears to us to be threatening. In this regard, Marie-Louise von Franz points out that the "new" often enters our lives lefthandedly. (The Latin for *left* is *sinister*. Renewal often appears initially as something sinister.)

A Skunk That Stinks of Garlic

In actual fact we often behave as though the elements we refuse to recognize in our personalities didn't exist. We recognize that the unconscious is alive, but we don't acknowledge that our repressed emotions find circuitous channels to express themselves. Paul's experience provides a good illustration of this theme:

Paul was forty when he started therapy. His mother and father had possessed relatively adequate parenting skills. His father was proud of his wife and worked hard in his career; he was a "good-boy" type. Paul's mother came from a comfortable family that rejected her because they disapproved of the man she chose to marry. Paul's parents had three children, and although things started out smoothly for the family, tragedy lay in wait for them.

When Paul was three years old the family house was completely destroyed by fire; this left them in extreme poverty. His parents and their three children were reduced to living in a one-room apartment; the parents slept on the sofa, the youngest child on the table, and the other two children on chairs. During the day the front part of the room also served as the father's office.

The most tragic consequence of this event was Paul's mother sinking into a terrible depression. She, who used to spend the whole day singing like a lark, sewing for her children, taking pride in keeping them clean and well dressed, now began to let everything fall to pieces. The children had to make extreme efforts to adapt; they could no longer recognize themselves in the dark mirror of their mother. The following year Paul was sent to a boarding school run by nuns who maintained discipline by any means. When Paul's mother didn't come to visit him, the nuns told him it was because he hadn't been good enough. He therefore deeply repressed all his aggressive inclinations, stifled his anger at being abandoned, and tried to adapt to his new, hostile surroundings.

Since he was intelligent, Paul did well at school. He had tremendous difficulty later, though, in adapting to his work environment. During the time he was in therapy he lost two important jobs. He simply couldn't manage to work. The lack of love in his childhood and his feelings of anger and rejection from those early years, left him desperately seeking emotional recognition in the workplace; this desperation made him unpopular at work. He could only work if he felt loved, but the confidence and respect he needed he could only gain once he had proved his competence.

A detail from the beginning of Paul's sessions with me that I had neglected to address when it came up finally led us to his issues of repressed aggression and the indirect ways it finds expression. During that early phase in his therapy, Paul had reeked of garlic; when he left my office I would have to open the windows to get rid of the stench. I had avoided talking to him about it at that time. A dream of his finally cleared the air.

I was showing my apartment to a girl. In the apartment there was a mother skunk who hung her babies on the clothing of everyone who passed by. The baby skunks had little hooks on their backs.

This dream of Paul's finally gave me a chance to broach the delicate subject of his garlic problem but I certainly never imagined this investigation would be quite so productive! To my great surprise, Paul stated of his own accord that garlic was his way of imposing himself on others. At work, he wanted to be accepted even if he didn't work; in therapy, he wanted to be accepted even if he reeked of garlic. As it turned out, this business of bad odors had a long history for Paul. One episode occurred in his hippie days when he took pleasure in never washing, even though it bothered the other people in the commune. He also confessed that his poor personal hygiene was one of the major complaints of the woman who had left him seven years earlier. In the end, this all went back to his mother's depression. In one day, the woman had lost all interest in keeping her children and her house clean.

Paul's adult behavior was a repressed form of protest against his mother; it expressed his anger at having been neglected. He was looking constantly for someone who would love him unconditionally. He refused to admit that his childhood was over, that no one now owed him that kind of love. At the same time he felt guilty about imposing himself on others through his extreme behaviors. He therefore tried to gain forgiveness by showing his extreme willingness to help others. Occasionally he even risked his life in this endeavor; once he agreed to deliver a girlfriend's parcel to the post office in a raging snowstorm, even though he had faulty brakes and no windshield wipers.

Internal rage and anger make themselves felt in convoluted ways when the conscious self denies them acknowledgment. An individual can fall prey to forces within him that always surface in unpleasant ways and may block his development.

MEETING THE PRIMITIVE MAN

When Aggression "Has" Us

Paul smells of garlic, Roger breaks into a smile, Tony stays always on his guard. All three of them are worried their aggression will all come spilling out. Of course it does come spilling out, but only when the situation is not too dangerous. It spills out in inappropriate ways; it is directed against an object, or a garage mechanic, or a therapist with a delicate sense of smell. These three case histories show us that repressing active energies is not an effective solution. Whether he wants to or not, every man must encounter the shadow he carries within him. He must immerse himself in his own primitive origins. He must liberate Iron Hans. Developing awareness of the shadow seems to me the only possible way for a man to master the potentially beneficial power of his aggression. After all, we can only control what we know intimately, in our guts, in the deep recesses of our heart.

Here are Jung's thoughts about this subject. He comments here on Job's anger against God:

> *It is far better to admit the affect and submit to its violence than to try to escape it by all sorts of intellectual tricks or by emotional value judgments. Although, by giving way to the affect, one imitates all the bad qualities of the outrageous act that provoked it and thus makes oneself guilty of the same fault, that is precisely the point of the whole proceeding: the violence is meant to penetrate to a man's vitals, and he to*

succumb to its action. He must be affected by it, otherwise its
full effect will not reach him. But he should know, or learn to
know, what has affected him, for in this way he transforms the
blindness of the violence on the one hand and of the affect on
the other into knowledge.[3]

A man who lacked a father, and consequently repressed his
own aggression, must learn to tame the primitive man within
himself. The things we refuse to accept about ourselves always
show up on the outside, sometimes in tragic forms. Divorces,
car accidents, bankruptcies, firings: all sorts of violent occur-
rences assail us when we refuse to recognize them as parts of
ourselves. The bad guy within us goes right on with his
insidious business, while we go on, outside, laughing or
crying.

This bad guy roams freely in our unconscious because we
have denied him entry to our consciousness. Furthermore, his
energy has the power to possess us because we repress it. None
of us wants to be a cold-blooded killer or a ferocious tiger;
but our natural aggression has become perverted because we
have rejected its power instead of finding an acceptable channel
for it. Because we refuse to "have" aggression, aggression
"has" us. Whenever we are frustrated, the brute in us takes
over with his verbal violence, physical violence, extreme coldness toward others, thoughts of suicide, and so forth. Freud's
powerful id will find a way to express itself; it will come
spilling out whether we like it or not.

Men must become aware of their aggressive nature, but their
awareness must enable them to control and *master this power*. I
do not encourage men to behave more violently, but I do
encourage them to embrace their internal energy as a way of
becoming more comfortable with themselves. Acknowledging
the primitive man who slumbers in the unconscious is a

---

3. Carl Gustav Jung, *Psychology and Religion: West and East*, Collected
Works, vol. 11, Series XX (Princeton, N.J.: Princeton University Press,
1956), p. 562.

necessary stage in their quest for personal autonomy, self-affirmation, and inner security.

Awareness of this power does not lead to violence; repression of it does. Most killers and rapists report impulses they just can't resist. In a sense, they too are victims, attacked by their own inner violence. Most cases of domestic violence get started in this way: a feeling of inadequacy or hopelessness suddenly expresses as an urge to hit somebody; the urge is overwhelming, like a bolt of lightning; the individual becomes totally subject to its irrational power. The ego is not able to withstand the assault of this internal force, and the individual is compelled to act out in order to release the unbearable tension. Afterwards, the individual looks back on his violence with a kind of horror, but he goes right on hiding it in his unconscious—until the next outburst of verbal abuse or the next round of blows and beatings.

How to Open Iron Hans's Cage

How can we transform aggressive energy that expresses itself only in acts of hostility or internal rage? How can we turn it into something healthy? How can we provoke a catharsis that expresses our violence and our negative feelings, and at the same time empowers us with the healthy energy of our aggression? I believe the answer is to create special places and moments in which we can tap into our repressed emotions and contain them in symbolic forms; the answer is to push ourselves in our fantasies as far as we can into our emotional impulses so that we can learn what's there and how it's affecting us. Here is an example of this process:

Alex is a deceptively mild-mannered young man in his early twenties. He has a lot of repressed aggression, thoughts of suicide, and unsuccessful experiences in his love relationships. His complaints focus mainly on the character of his mother, which he describes as "too strong." From time to time I encourage him to push himself to the limits of the anger he feels toward her, but he always resists. One day, though, he finally got in touch with his aggression:

With a mixture of laughter and tears he allowed himself to break the taboo and give in to his rage. The following image then emerged: in the basement of the family home he hacks his mother to death with an axe and then stomps on her bloody remains in a sort of dance of jubilation.

For Alex this imagining was a radical experience. He finally went to the end of his negative feelings and reached the sadistic murderer within him. The experience calmed him. The negative feelings that had governed him before gradually found expression in more realistic forms. His hatred of his mother transformed into an appreciation of all she had done for him. And little by little he rediscovered his enjoyment of life. Alex learned an important lesson about acting out symbolically.

Why does this symbolic process work? It worked for Alex because his complaints were not directed against his real mother, but against his mother complex. A complex is a psychological entity, and it must be combatted on psychological ground. Murdering his mother symbolized his separating from his internal mother. Alex plunged into his aggressive energies and put their positive potential to use. Killing his real mother wouldn't have brought him anything, except the dubious privilege of spending the rest of his life in jail.

There are other more concrete rituals than this imaginary violence in use in the world. In Ghana, for instance, people dance in a circle around a mask representing the violent transgressor. They affirm that every man carries this potential for violence within him; they exorcise that potential by dancing day and night to the beat of drums. I recently took a group of men on a daylong outdoor workshop. I had them exhaust themselves by going to the limits of their physical endurance; their exhaustion helped them rediscover their physical spontaneity and shed their conditioning and their constant self-control. All of this put them in closer touch with the tribal, organic side of themselves.

In order to transform aggression into self-knowledge, it is necessary to admit the fantasy world, to accept our inner workings without judgment. These are the first steps on the road to intimacy. Provided we experience them intensely and emotionally, these awakened dreams and active imaginings can be profound psychological experiences, genuine "events" in our lives. They reduce the chance that we will spring into action blindly. The meeting with his shadow gives a man substance; it defines him. Experiencing fully his feelings gives him a foothold in the reality of the world and its violence. The shadow bestows on him a choice and a duty concerning his repressed hostility: since he has learned where it goes and how far it can lead him, he is now responsible for it.

A Man Is Not a Man Until . . .

A man is not a man until he has accessed his raw, untamed energy and taken pleasure in his capacity to fight and defend himself. Only then can he transform his blind rage into the power to commit himself, to handle tensions, and to make difficult decisions. A feeling of inner security also develops; it is based on his realization that, whatever happens to go wrong, he can get help from his inner resources, from the basic energy of his aggression.

Getting in touch with Iron Hans' masculine dynamism and mastering that power, is what enables a man to penetrate the world of women, literally and figuratively. As long as a man believes cloying sweetness or blind violence is his only means of defending himself, he cannot enjoy a complete relationship with a woman. Before he can give himself up to the intimacy of the couple, he must be able to survive rejection or he must make the break himself if that proves necessary.

THE INNER WARRIOR

The Romans made a god of the warrior Mars. They recognized him as a basic psychological force; they devoted themselves to his cult. Mars represents confrontations, insults, blows that define limits and trigger hostilities. He is also one who can decide things, cut through them, and slam the door as he leaves. There is much more to Mars than just that, though: Mars is also a very important psychological activator. He gets things moving; he provokes confrontations and jolts us out of our stagnation. Mars is a vital force, a thunderbolt, an awakener. He is the springtime that shakes the world out of its torpor.

In a lecture presented at the C. G. Jung Circle in Montreal in May, 1987,[4] the analyst James Hillman spoke about the civilized aspects of the martial arts versus uncontrolled aggressive impulses. Mars of course lives in discipline, in the same precision and concentration that handling weapons requires. He has had to master his fear and learn respect for the power of his adversaries. He follows a moral code based on the ethics of warfare. Although he knows how to declare war, he also knows how to put an end to it and make peace. Mars also has a voluptuous side, which shows up in his beautiful attire, the braid on his uniforms, his gleaming weapons, the accoutrements of his horses. While he must often wallow in the mud and blood of the battlefield, he also enjoys moments of glory and brilliance. Our childlike enthusiasm for military parades testifies to this aspect of him. We like the handsome uniforms, the music of fifes and drums, the glint and glamor of metal shining in the sun. We succumb to Mars's charm, our eyes wide with admiration for this proud, disciplined divinity.

Nowadays, however, the warrior archetype is changing. Mars has to evolve, since the future of the planet requires it. A man can now be a warrior without ever striking a physical blow. The fight for a cleaner environment is a new battlefield for Mars, as is the struggle for peace in the world, and the campaign for human rights.

---

4. James Hillman, *L'amour de la guerre* ("The Love of War"), (Montreal: Cahiers du Cercle C. G. Jung de Montreál), May 1987.

Some Native American tribes provide exemplary models of warrior societies informed by respect for animal and plant life and awareness of the world's wholeness. These tribes did not exhaust their environment; they adapted to it and settled in it. We, in today's society, have tamed the external natural world, but our inner natural world is still a primitive place. We need to return to our origins; we need to cultivate the historical, mythical image of the Native American, living with respect for the laws of nature and the values of the spirit.

The world is becoming more psychologically aware and Mars is becoming "psychologized" too. Needs for brilliant exploits, tests of strength, and ordeals of self-control have all become internalized; they awaken the warrior within us. Taking up these challenges can create an intensity and involvement that makes our lives truly fulfilling. Awakening the inner warrior means awakening the pride and sparkle in us. An awakened Mars can help us overcome our bad habits, our physical or intellectual laziness. He can help us rediscover our vital passion for life.

An awakened Mars is a rush of springtime within us. To burst with health is a psychological and physiological experience within everyone's reach. The rush of springtime in us also brings the rush of love; responding to the spark of life makes us happy with ourselves and infatuated with life itself. In the Roman myths, Mars is, after all, the lover of Venus, the goddess of love and the most beautiful woman on Olympus. Venus loves Mars's intensity, his ardor for life. He brings her the vital spark that illuminates her in all her glory. It may seem a strange marriage this, a strange coming together of the fires of love and the flames of war, but Mars is so moved by his love for Venus that he lays down his arms. He no longer has to fight. He can shed his defenses, strip himself bare, and live in love. The mythical child born of his union with Venus was named Harmony.

The warrior can become an inner companion to our harmonizing with physical and psychological laws, and our cultural and natural environments. Mars, the awakener of life, knows the road to life because he is the very essence of life's vital energy. He knows that the road to harmony passes through love. An endeavor undertaken without love, or an intensity devoid of pleasure, cannot lead to harmony. Impulsive warriors that never lay down their arms, that never experience the sweetness and voluptuousness of life, can never attain their goals. Blind impulse will never bring us to the supreme joy of shining with all our glory in harmony with the impulsive life that flows through our veins.

Fighting to give the best of oneself—experiencing the best of oneself—is the very source of inner peace and self-love. Venus waits eternally for the awakened man within us, she welcomes him with all her charms and all her beauty. For the awakened man, nature reveals her full splendor; the world becomes for him a source of wonder, delight, and ecstasy. Venus takes him in her arms and the Warrior becomes Love.

At the height of our ardor, Venus comes to enrapture our bodies and minds; she brings mental states of great happiness and deep feelings of harmony; she takes us a long way from all the moral and intellectual gymnastics of preachings about universal love. Love exists only when the warrior has been awakened; only through the awakened Mars can harmony be attained. We can spend our whole lives preaching to ourselves and to others about the meaning of love, but as long as we go on doing nothing but sitting in front of the television with a big meal in our bellies, nothing will happen: life will remain empty of meaning. It will also be empty of meaning for our partners. Our partners will be living with men who lack vitality. When we give the best of ourselves, though, when we awaken our vigor and our pleasure, when we transcend ourselves, we find the inner Venus and the external Venus as well, the love that lies waiting for us in our partners.

"Woman, it is you to whom desire leads, all desire. Keep yourself for love, keep love itself, be loving in love and even before love, be open and ready for love. Rejoice, for you hold the filter and the secret. Rejoice, for you have been chosen to live in love.

"Man, strive to make yourself lovable, affirm your being and your body until you shine with incomparable brightness. Then Woman will open unto you and you will kindle in her the fire of love, and you will be bathed, drowned in her vast secret, and it will be delight, utter delight. Rejoice, Man, for although she is the one who holds the secret and the love, you are the one who sets love aflame, it is you who blazes with desire, it is you who makes love."[5]

5. Leclerc, *Hommes et femmes*, pp. 63–64.

FIVE

The Blood of the Father

BETRAYING THE BODY

The Wound of the Fisher King

The psychological problem of the past few generations of men actually has roots reaching back to the very foundations of Western civilization. The wounded masculine identity is not a recent phenomenon. From the moment dualist philosophy first made its appearance with the Greeks, and perhaps even before, it imposed a separation between body and mind, object and subject, nature and culture.

The masculine dilemma cannot ultimately be solved simply by reevaluating male aggressiveness and redirecting the warrior's vital intensity. This process is nicely illustrated by the story of Percival, one of the most extraordinary heroes of the Middle Ages. In his story we see the tragic consequences of constructing masculinity entirely in the outside world and the resulting loss of man's inner identity. There is no better symbol of external masculinity than the knight's armor, which provides a strong structure for the man inside and can even stand upright on its own.

There are many versions of the Percival or Parsifal legend,

from Chrétien de Troyes' medieval classic *Perceval ou le Conte de Graal (Percival or the Holy Grail)* to the John Boorman film *Excalibur*. First written down more than five hundred years ago, the story remains astonishingly modern in its implications. It certainly does away with any ideas we might have had of an idyllic past in which every son had a father, and there were no problems of masculine identity.

Young Percival lives alone with his mother; he never knew his father, who died at war. His brothers, too, perished in battle. Fearing the loss of her only remaining son, Percival's mother forbids him to pursue the ideals of chivalry. Nevertheless, he leaves her to make a chivalric journey, whereupon his mother dies of a broken heart. As he journeys, Percival charms a young maiden whose suitor, the Scarlet Knight, challenges him to a duel. Percival kills the knight, steals his shining red armor, and puts it on over the peasant clothes his mother lovingly sewed for him. He then proceeds on his way, leaving the damsel behind.

This incident sets the groundwork for Percival's search for masculine identity. His confrontation with the Scarlet Knight, whose armor is the color of blood and passion, represents an individual's initial confrontation with the world of instinct, the world of his own instinctive urges. He conquers these impulses by brute force, but this repression by force actually works against a genuine appropriation of the scarlet knight's virility. Although on the outside Percival displays the ostentatious, flamboyant, macho masculinity symbolized by his new armor, on the inside he is still a mommy's boy, since underneath he still wears the soft clothes his mother made for him.[1]

Percival in his new armor is presented to the court of King

---

1. My interpretation of this legend owes a great deal to a brilliant lecture and seminar entitled "Masculine Archetypes," presented by the Swiss analyst Bernard Sartorius at the C. G. Jung Circle in Montreal, May 1986. An excellent summary and differing interpretation of the legend can be found in Robert A. Johnson, *He: Understanding Masculine Psychology* (New York: Harper and Row, 1977).

Arthur and the Knights of the Round Table. There he is instructed in the arts of chivalry: how to wield weapons properly and how to ride a horse. Once his initiation is completed, he sets out to conquer the world.

He delivers a kingdom from the siege of a vicious tyrant and in return is offered the hand of a princess named Blanchefleur. The marriage has barely been consummated when, lured by dreams of further conquests, Percival abandons his wife—just as he abandoned his mother and the Scarlet Knight's maiden. Obviously, Percival is unable to commit himself to women. His adventures always draw him away from involvement with the feminine world. His obsessive pursuit of male heroism and his fierce independence with regard to women finally bring Percival face to face with the mystery of the Holy Grail.

One day he comes to a lake. In the middle of the lake he notices a man who is fishing, perfectly motionless. This turns out to be the Fisher King, who eagerly invites the knight to a banquet in his castle that evening. In the middle of the banquet something very strange occurs. The hero witnesses a procession culminating in the mysterious spectacle of a lance dripping blood into a chalice: the chalice of the Holy Grail.

Percival is dumbstruck. He wants very badly to ask for an explanation but doesn't dare to because he promised his mother he would always hold his tongue in society. His need for silence proves unfortunate: when the banquet is over he learns that the Fisher King is suffering from a wound in the thigh area, and that this wound will not heal until a guest breaks the silence by asking about the strange spectacle he has witnessed. Percival also learns that the author of the king's wound is a treacherous witch. The bleeding lance is the same one with which the Roman centurion pierced the side of Christ on the Cross.

High Versus Low, Feminine Versus Masculine

Let us pause at this point and consider some of the legend's various elements. Many of its implications are still relevant today: the central dilemma of men's silence, for instance, and the fragility of masculine identity symbolized by the king's wound.

The king's wound signifies that masculinity's governing principle has become afflicted. The location of his wound is described in vague terms: "in the area of the thigh." In other words, it is near the middle of the body, at the level of the lower abdomen or the genitals. This region divides the upper and lower body: it separates the "noble" parts, namely the heart, lungs, and head, from the so-called "inferior" parts, the stomach and the sexual organs. The obscure description of the king's wound can be seen as a veiled reference to castration: the principle of male reproduction has been damaged, the masculine has lost the power to engender or regenerate. It is interesting to note that in another version of the legend, the thrust of the spear comes not from a treacherous witch but from a Mohammedan—and it is specified that the king was wounded in his genitals.

The Fisher King's wound in the middle part of his body indicates that masculine energy has been cut in two: the noble, higher parts have been severed from the base, lower parts. The masculine is unable to regenerate itself, unable to engender new attitudes, and unable to progress at all since it has been cut off from its own legs. It has lost contact with the earth; it is ungrounded.

A witch is said to have delivered the offending thrust of the spear. Witches represent the feminine principle that men reject. The feminine principle then becomes malevolent and turns against men. Percival's meeting with the Fisher King comes after the knight has abandoned his wife, Blanchefleur. The wound, then, reflects men's ambiguous attitudes toward women: it is as though men have dissociated themselves from what they think is the repulsive side of their nature and have then projected this repulsive side onto women. Men's attempt to keep women in an inferior position leads to the anger of the feminine element and its ultimate revenge.

The spear as the agent of the king's wound reinforces the symbol of the bleeding lance. There is a connection between the witch's spear and the Roman soldier's pike. Christ's wound is linked to the king's wound and to men's inadequate integration of feminine elements.

It can be argued that the reference to the blood of Christ implies that the basic premises of the Christian religion, despite their civilizing influence, are both wounded and wounding. Christianity makes a strong division between the upper and the lower; instead of uniting mind and instinct, it separates them. The Christian world cultivates an ethereal, sky-blue spirituality; it refuses a place in the world of the spirit to instinct and substance. Instinctive, "red" spirituality is denied, and women are left to bear the burden of this division of the masculine. The rituals of witches, with their weird dances and plentiful sexual allusions, can be viewed as compensations for this blindness of established Christianity.

The Native American religions, which many consider primitive, do not seem to suffer these divisions. Titles such as Great Manitou and Great Spirit do not reflect a disincarnated spiritual principle. On the contrary, they maintain their natural resonances, and we can sense in them the flight of the eagle, the roll of thunder, or the rush of the wind. Collections of Native American spiritual writings like *Barefoot on the Sacred Earth* embrace the whole of humankind and the entire cosmos. In comparison, "Our Father who art in heaven" seems quite disincarnated. When the tops of our bodies are cut off from the bottoms, we lose our vital contact with the sacred earth and wound what is feminine in us.

In attempting to tame the powerful impulses of sex and violence, Christianity (a religion dominated by men) has lost sight of the essential need for an instinctual spirituality that harms neither man's relationship with his instincts nor his relationship with the world of nature. Two thousand years later we see that many of the things foreshadowed in *Percival or the Holy Grail* are now taking place. It has taken the women's movement, the sexual revolution, and the pollution of the planet to show men that their conception of the world is unhealthy. Deep in the Middle Ages, Chrétien de Troyes no doubt had only a vague notion of the drama of masculine identity, yet he provided an accurate picture of it in the chivalrous character, Percival. Is it significant that the author died before he could finish writing this romance?

One final element in Percival's story is worthy of attention: the silence surrounding the bleeding lance and the king's loss of vitality. The king never mentions his wound to Percival, and Percival does not dare to ask questions about the spectacle of the bleeding lance—it is as if these events were so impressive and so disturbing that they have to be repressed. This silence of the polite young man trying to please his mother prevents the solving of the problems in the kingdom. As Bernard Sartorius puts it, "He had to stop behaving 'correctly' in order to behave adequately at another level."[2] In order to behave adequately at another level and still respect his total being, a man needs his instincts; he cannot leave them behind with his umbrella in the vestibule. Men's silence about what is undermining their masculinity keeps them stuck in a quagmire.

In Boorman's film, the king's illness is linked to the scourges that are wreaking havoc on the land: drought, crop failure, plague, and barbarism. Life itself has fallen ill because of men's silence and lack of involvement. Sky blue, heavenly spirituality has led to a disincarnation and abandonment of earthly things. Percival can cure the king, though, by asking a simple question, making his own voice heard, confronting the problem. In the same way, we can heal our own disincarnated masculinity and the problems it has engendered. It is time for us to speak, to tend to our internal division by again becoming one with our external environment. It is time we rediscovered what the Taoists and alchemists have always taught:

2. Sartorius, *Les Archetypes*.

Heaven above, Heaven below
stars above, stars below
all that is above is also below
know this and rejoice.[3]

Percival, after all, is not uninitiated. His training in King Arthur's court enabled him to refine his masculinity. He learned to tame and master himself, and he has become virile. There is something lacking though in this kind of initiation with its emphasis on the heroic type of male, all armor and appearances. Such masculinity is constructed entirely on the outside, and in this sense Percival's initiation is the prototype of male initiation that has prevailed ever since. Men have learned not to cry; they are supposed to be disciplined, competitive, triumphant. These are indeed basic, necessary stages in male psychological development, but men seem to have left something else behind as we emerged from the tribal world into the so-called civilized world. The following pages will suggest what it is we have lost, as they examine the initiation rites for teenage boys practised by some of the original peoples of the Earth.

IN THE ENTRAILS OF THE EARTH

Tribal Initiation

As I mentioned in the opening chapter, elaborate rituals for the initiation of young males were widespread among tribal peoples. These rites helped teenage boys to become true sons of their fathers. They marked an official separation from the mother and made the adolescent into a man.

According to the anthropologist Victor Turner, initiation represents an interstructural stage between one social structure

---

3. Hermes Trimegistus, "Tabula smaragdina," quoted by C. G. Jung in *Psychology and Alchemy*, Collected Works, vol. 12, Bollingen Series XX, 2nd ed. (Princeton, N.J.: Princeton University Press, 1968), p. 77.

and the structure that will replace it; it represents, to be more precise, a marginal period, of "liminality" between the two. For the tribe, the initiates symbolically cease to exist. They become invisible and are referred to in the third person even when they are present. They are considered to be androgynous or sexless as though they were corpses or foetuses. They are covered with lime, mud, or ash, to symbolize their return to the earth and to the world of the dead. They have to die in one state so that they can be reborn in another. Incidentally, the same emphasis on dirtiness has been preserved in college initiations and stag parties, although its deeper significance has now been lost.

The initiate represents the outer limit of society; he is temporarily shunted aside before he is readmitted with his new identities. In this sense the initiate actually becomes a new person; in future he will refer to his childhood self as if he were talking about someone else. The adolescent rite of passage is modeled on human biological processes such as birth and death. The ritual provides an external, visible form for a process that is internal and conceptual. The initiation symbols "are, in many societies, drawn from the biology of death, decomposition, catabolism, and other physical processes that have a negative tinge, such as menstruation (frequently regarded as the absence or loss of a fetus). . . . The neophyte may be buried, forced to lie motionless in the posture of a corpse, may be stained black, or may be forced to live for a while in the company of masked and monstrous mummers representing, inter alia, the dead, or worse, the undead. The metaphor of dissolution is often applied to neophytes; they are allowed to go filthy, and they are identified with the earth, the generalized matter into which every specific individual returns . . ."[4]

---

4. Victor Turner, *The Forest of Symbols*, quoted by Jan O. Stein and Murray Stein in "Psychotherapy, Initiation and the Midlife Crisis," in *Betwixt and Between: Patterns of Masculine and Feminine Initiation* (LaSalle, Ill.: Open Court, 1987), p. 292.

This emphasis on natural, biological processes connected with the earth and with human metabolism stands in sharp contrast to the initiation rituals Percival underwent. His initiations involved only his hunter/warrior side; they completely bypassed the realities of his body and his involvement with the substance of the world.

We know that the initiation of hunters took place inside the earth. The late mythologist Joseph Campbell believed that the drawings in prehistoric caves such as Lascaux and Pech-Merle served as instruction manuals: the scenes painted on the cavern walls taught neophytes how to hunt and kill animals, the lords of the earth, with awe and respect.[5]

In tribal initiations, dirtiness is an essential part of the ritual. Compared to initiations with dry swords and armor, tribal initiations are wet. Here we find an explanation for the bleeding lance in the Grail legend: what is dry, sharp, and masculine must be soaked in the wetness of blood and decomposition in order to be reborn. Because they can neither menstruate or give birth to children, men have a greater need to get in touch with the natural biological processes of death and rebirth.

Our modern culture clearly shows how necessary these rites of passage are—and the spiritual catastrophe that occurs when they are lost. Without knowing it, today's adolescents of both sexes repeat these same initiatory patterns: the androgynous appearance, the monstrous hairstyles and outrageous accessories, the carefully torn or tattered clothes, and the deliberate neglect of cleanliness and hygiene. This behavior expresses an unconscious need for initiation, but unfortunately fathers of these adolescents do not seem to understand this need. Young people in our culture, like those in tribal cultures, must go through a transition, an initiatory stage; they must explore the limits of their future identities.

In a society based like ours is on spectacles and appearances,

5. Joseph Campbell and Bill Moyers, *The Power of Myth* (New York: Doubleday, 1988), p. 81.

initiation for young people means nothing more than their passively imitating various superstars. Our ancestral initiation has been emptied of its content and of its participation in the sacred meaning of the universe. Traditional ordeals of initiation intended to instill this sense of participation in the flesh of the novice.

From Puberty to Manhood: Mutilation

The fact that some tribal initiations include mutilation of the body is a disturbing reality. Writers on the subject affirm that the fathers of the tribe perform the mutilations in a way that is both gentle and cruel, but the apparent barbarity of it offends our modern sensibilities. Does mutilation serve only to reinforce fathers' authority over their sons? What is its psychological role?

The goal of initiation is to buttress the masculine ego. Ritual mutilation is an expression of submission to the male principle. The initiate's submission to suffering imposed by his father must be seen as an act of masculine love signifying the death of the mommy's boy. The pain of mutilation expresses the pain the initiate feels when he severs his links with his mother. Mutilation establishes contact for the initiate with the earthy, savage, masculine elements that come from the depths of the earth.

As the philosopher Gustave Thibon states, "The law is inexorable: we lessen our own suffering to the extent that we weaken our inner direct communion with reality."[6] Stephen Shapiro adds that "Men who remain unable to suffer remain puerile, exiled from the reality of human contact and from concern about the world they inherit."[7] This says a lot about our constant search for comfort!

I spoke earlier of Bob the hero who, although he had a successful international acting career, still had feelings of ex-

6. Gustave Thibon, quoted by Stephen A. Shapiro, *Manhood*, p. 66.
7. Shapiro, *Manhood*, p. 66.

treme loneliness. He suffered from his loss of contact with reality. Alienated from all love relationships, he felt there was no longer any meaning to his life. I concluded that he had totally cut off from his feelings and had taken complete refuge in his head. I therefore encouraged him to let his emotions flow freely. He then visualized the image of a hermaphroditic man who had been flayed alive, bound in chains, and hung on steel wires over a void. After describing this image, he broke into tears: he had finally made contact with his own suffering. Bob later discovered that by accepting his feelings and his own suffering, he returned to the communion with others that he had lost. This discovery cheered him up immeasurably; it benefitted his acting technique. His world recovered its meaning.

Whether it is imposed on us or by us, suffering is a basic fact of existence. We never question the pleasures that come our way, but we always have trouble accepting the things that hurt us. Mutilation by tribal fathers is an attempt to give meaning to this inevitable dimension of human life. Tribal fathers are aware that suffering cannot always be avoided and that the sacrifice it represents is one of the structural elements of the cosmos.

For all its apparent brutality, tribal mutilation expresses a very simple truth: to become genuine human beings, we must open to a world of unforeseen circumstances in which we will be spared nothing. It is almost as though human substance must be corrupted and punctured so that its essence can emerge. Although the son's unconscious, unified world of childhood is in fact burst assunder in the initiation, the purpose of the initiation is not merely to gain entry for him into a world that is absurd; the goal is to provide him entry into a wider unity, a larger universe. He becomes a full-fledged participant in, and a responsible member of the community. His actions now carry their own weight in the continuation of the world.

The major difference between the mutilation of the Fisher

King and the mutilation of tribal initiates is that the former is passive while the latter is voluntary. The Fisher King suffers from a wound to his self-esteem that was treacherously inflicted on him; initiatory mutilations are performed according to ritual. Tribal mutilations transmit a meaning that goes beyond both the mutilator and the mutilated. Ancestral rites of passage reflect the basic laws of the psyche that requires the ego to sacrifice its blind exclusivity and open up to the universe.

When a young man sheds his passive and dependent attitudes, he has to face up to another aspect of reality. Learning to tolerate suffering and to inflict it when necessary is a way of bursting the cozy bubble of dependency that we all try to construct around ourselves. Mutilation signifies violent contact with the reality of the universe—contact that men otherwise often escape as long as they live under the watchful gaze of their mothers.

Born in the Blood of the Father

The role of the initiators is to conduct young adolescents through the transition from puberty to adulthood, to explain, to transmit, and give them the experience of being a man. The Australian aborigines, for example, re-enact the initiate's original birth. They build a tunnel of branches and bushes, 20 or 30 feet in length, and require the boy to go into it. After a great deal of shouting and commotion, the initiate emerges from the other end of the tunnel, where he is welcomed with open arms and solemnly declared to be a man. He has been reborn through the body of man; he now possesses a new mind and a new body.[8]

Whereas a man's first birth is nourished by his mother's

8. Adapted from comments by Robert Bly, "Initiations masculines contemporaines" ("Contemporary Masculine Initiations"), translated from the English by Jean-Guy Girouard, *Guides-Ressources*, vol. 4., no. 2, Montreal, Nov./Dec. 1988, p. 29

milk, his second is a birth nourished by his father's blood. The elders of the Kikuyu tribe in Africa take on the role of male wet nurses: their boys sit in a circle with the tribal fathers, each of whom uses the same carefully sharpened knife to make a small cut in his arm and let a bit of his blood drop into a bowl. By drinking this blood, the adolescents become men.[9] Born in their mothers' milk, they are now reborn in their fathers' blood. What an impressive way to be welcomed into the male community!

The idea of a nursing father who gives birth with his body pinpoints one of the major deficiencies of our own culture: nowadays we are reborn only through the father's mind. We are initiated only into the spiritual dimensions of the father: his principles, laws, rules, and regulations. Because our fathers are absent, we ourselves become absent from our bodies; we become disincarnated walking heads, severed from physical sensations. We remain cut off from our bodies' vitality, from our blood; we are frightened of fleshy women. Our presence in our bodies, though, is the very foundation of our presence in the world.

To adopt a term used by the psychoanalyst Jean-Charles Crombez, the body is "transpersonal"; it has the same power as the mind to connect us with the universe. The need to survive in a difficult environment taught our ancient forebears that a man must make contact with the world through his feet, not only through his head. This lesson holds equally true for today's society: our sky blue spirituality needs enrichment from the "red" spirituality that comes from the depths of the earth.

After one of my lectures, a man in the audience got up and told us about a plan he had formulated with two or three others, all fathers of boys aged 12 to 16. They intended to get together around a campfire in the woods one afternoon, to talk to their sons about life, sex, the obstacles they themselves had encountered, and the joys they had known.

---

9. Ibid., p. 29.

Creating special, symbolic moments like this can help young males establish their identity. It makes them aware of the connection between themselves and their fathers. The fathers break their own habitual silence to share their thoughts and feelings with their sons. By demonstrating to the boys that they are worthy of this kind of attention, the fathers confirm their sons' status as men.

Words that share, reassure, reveal, and confirm—however brief they may be—are an essential part of this kind of initiatory experience. Remember Christ's words to his first apostle: "Thou art Peter, and upon this rock I will build my church." Breaking through silence, breaking through the father's constraint is an act of incalculable importance for the son. The eloquence of the words and the age of the participants are not important provided the words are true and not rigidly adherent to any particular principle. Unfortunately, for many men this opening up of the heart often happens only in extreme circumstances—at the bedside of a dying father, for instance. The task of the initiating father is not to lock himself into some artificial role as the perfect parent or the strict disciplinarian. On the contrary, only by sharing his imperfect humanity and removing the son's obligation to be a god or a devil can the father ease his son's entry into life.

SIX

Beneficial Depression

INITIATION HUNGER

Initiation opens a door to the world. In today's society, the father's absence is reflected in the lack of these rituals designed to help a young man make the transition from adolescence to adulthood. As a result, becoming a man now involves all sorts of painful contortions that we don't usually recognize as being part of the initiation process. Modern rites of passage are unconscious ones; they range from accidents to depression. Like traditional initiations, though, they break down our passive ideals and help us accept the things we fear or despise.

How Accidents, Divorces, Ulcers, and Bankruptcies Contribute to Male Initiation

Men decide to undergo analysis in most cases as a result of some dramatic event in their lives. One man has just been thrown out by his wife; she wants a divorce and he's worried about losing the house—or his mind. Another man has two car accidents in the same week. Yet another has developed ulcers from overwork. One fellow has been forced into bankruptcy; another is stunned to realize he has lost his sexual vitality.

Women consult an analyst because they feel something is amiss on the inside, but men—the eternal heroes who always think they can get out of it on their own—submit to analysis only when they experience a reversal of fate. When the crisis has reached a peak and everything is falling apart, they finally react. Often they secretly hope that therapy will let them recover without forcing them to ask questions about themselves. They bring their psyche to the garage expecting the analyst to repair it without much cost or pain. This attitude of theirs usually means it will take the analyst a long time to get them to realize they have played a part in their own misfortune and may in fact have unconsciously desired it. Upon closer examination, their accidents often turn out to be ways of putting an end to protracted adolescence. These various forms of misfortune—or mutilation—express an unconscious hunger for initiation. The role of therapy is to give meaning to men's suffering as a kind of initiation experience.[1]

One Man's Unconscious Initiation Hunger

Let's go back and take a closer look at the case of Julian.

Julian came to consult me after the birth of his first child, a son he was extremely proud of. Julian was 30 years old, an exceptionally pleasant and charming fellow who was well educated and well mannered. He was married to a woman his own age who had studied in the same field he did; very much aware of the needs of modern couples, he willingly shared half the domestic work with her.

Julian fled his bourgeois European family in his early twenties by immigrating to Quebec. He despised his father, who

---

1. I would like to note in passing that I have relied on the concept of initiation hunger developed by Anthony Stevens in his book *Archetypes, a Natural History of the Self;* see the chapter entitled "Personal Identity and the Stages of Life," pp. 140–174.

was extremely authoritarian and often away on business. His mother was a dependent, depressive woman who used her son as a confidant for her unhappiness and feelings about her husband's affairs.

Julian's wife, a competent and competitive person, obtained more contracts than he did, which left him feeling humiliated. He was troubled by sadistic sexual fantasies in which he would chain women up in a basement. In the first dream he told me about, he found himself sitting at the bedside of his wife: she was dead! He insisted nevertheless that their relationship was in good shape.

In the course of the next few months he felt increasingly abandoned; his feeling was exacerbated by all the attention his wife was giving to their son. When his frustration became unbearable, Julian started having fits of rage. At first he would destroy objects that belonged to him: a painting he liked, for example, or a bookshelf. Then he started breaking things in the kitchen. What began as simple exchanges of insults with his wife quickly led to the inevitable: on several occasions he hit his wife and threatened to commit suicide and kill their son if she spoke about it to anyone. Finally the couple separated.

I watched this escalation of violence helplessly from the sidelines. Where were these sudden attacks of fury coming from and why, with the best intentions in the world, was Julian unable to control them? Julian had broken off relations with his father and had served as his mother's personal confidant; he had become imprisoned in the maternal world. He couldn't stand the thought that his wife/mother might love someone else more than him.

There was a court hearing to decide custody of the child. The wife, wanting exclusive rights, exaggerated what had happened, describing Julian to the court as a pathologically violent man who would inevitably contaminate his child. In actual fact, Julian enjoyed an excellent relationship with his son. Because he was frightened of being labelled a wife beater,

Julian's first reflex had been not to tell his lawyer about his acts of violence at all. I found this silence unacceptable, and against all the rules of analysis, I told him so openly—and probably quite paternally. In my opinion, if he kept silent to save face, Julian would never overcome his guilt feelings and might well have to live with a psychological handicap for the rest of his days. I advised him to tell his lawyer the whole truth; he had to accept responsibility for what he had done even if it made him curl up with shame.

Julian's humiliation in admitting the shameful truth served as a symbolic mutilation that allowed him to break out of his adolescence. He was forced to admit he was not just a polite young man whom everyone admired: he was guilty, he had struck his wife. Eventually, after the court had conducted an investigation that confirmed his excellent relationship with his son, joint custody of the child was awarded.

During this same period, Julian began law school. I thought law school an excellent idea for him since it would let him satisfy his need for power in ways other than through violence. It also symbolically moved him closer to the world of his despised father. Law school requires enormous self-discipline and perseverance because the competition is so fierce, and Julian was too busy to pay much attention to his depressed moods and erotic fantasies. He also had a lot less time to indulge in interminable and often acrimonious telephone conversations with his ex-wife.

This transition to his father's world, was tremendously beneficial for Julian. He went through a difficult period of loneliness during which he came to recognize and accept his real needs in spite of the limits imposed on him by his emotional needs. For example, in choosing a new partner he needed to remember that he was terribly vulnerable and frightened of encroachments. He found the strength to finish his law degree and to develop a satisfying relationship with a new partner. Spending time with his son became a source of deep comfort for him, despite the heavy demands of child care. His confrontation with the law enabled him to break out of adolescence and learn to feel his own genuine needs.

What Solitude Can Teach Us

It is worth noting how Julian's self-imposed solitude turned out to be a formative experience. In this regard, the analyst Jerome Bernstein maintains that unless a man has developed the capacity to live alone and build himself a nest, he cannot live with a woman without making her into his mother, that is, depending on her in a maternal sense. Psychologically, a man needs to feel he owns an internal home. Otherwise he will require his partners to provide him with one.[2]

In cultural terms we live in an extroverted society that has little room for solitude and silence. We constantly stuff ourselves with conversations, films, theater, radio, video, or television. Always worried about missing something important, we have become cultural and political bulimics, binging on information and entertainment. We gorge on whatever happens to be available, just so we won't have to remain alone with ourselves.

Quite a few of my patients are incapable of spending a few hours alone without falling into a depression. One of them confessed that spending a day in the country alone had become a truly heroic act for him. These men are frightened of the solitude and silence that threaten their dependence; they do not want to be weaned; they are afraid of falling into a void. Solitude can be instructive, though. An individual may well discover resources within himself that he wasn't previously aware of. Solitude initiates in the sense that it forces an individual to confront and overcome his own unhappiness. Medieval monks claimed that remaining alone in their cells taught them everything they needed to know.

---

2. Jerome S. Bernstein, "The Decline of Masculine Rites of Passage in Our Culture: The Impact on Masculine Individuation," *Betwixt and Between: Patterns of Masculine and Feminine Initiation,* p. 140.

Maria's Fever

Let me provide a second example of how a personal crisis can become initiatory. This one is taken from my personal life. In 1974, after several years of working in the professional theater, I decided to go back to school and get training to be an analyst. At this time I had a dream that made a deep impression on me. I called it "The Maria Dream," and this is how it went:

> *I was at the school where I boarded and studied. I was lined up with the other students. We had just come out of study class and were about to write an exam. We were all wearing navy blue blazers and gray pants. Suddenly, for no reason, I bolted from the group and escaped through a side door. Everything was pitch black outside, and there was a sort of crazy excitement in the air. I soon found myself in the depths of the earth, at the bottom of huge crevasses that formed immense corridors through the rock. I was carrying a torch and leading a troop of men. We were walking quickly as if it were some sort of emergency. The atmosphere was like that of a revolution. Every time we met another group of men, everyone would shout "Maria," like a password. Suddenly I found myself alone at the entrance to a well-lit gallery. There was a little stream running through it and an old woman was fetching water for Maria who was lying there on the earth. Maria was sick, racked with a very high fever. I bent over her and when I got up I had the face of Rudolph Valentino.*

I was moved by the energy and touching simplicity of the dream. It made me aware of my unwell feminine component: my anima had a high fever. Just as I was about to embark on a difficult program of studies, it was signaling its opposition to my typically male ideals that left no room for the feminine. I could make contact with Maria only after running away from the traditional male values associated with the boarding school.

The dream impressed me but it didn't make me change my plans: I went on with my studies. Two years later, at the end of my first year at the C. G. Jung Institute in Zurich, I fell gravely ill. Maria's fever took the form of ulcerative colitis, an acute inflammation of the intestine. This is a chronic disease requiring lifelong medication; it also indicates a serious risk of colon cancer. By this time, I had long since forgotten the Maria dream. My illness continued to flare up whenever I went through periods of great stress. One attack in the fall of 1985 lasted five months, during which I lost blood many times a day. I had built up a resistance to the medication and my condition was seriously deteriorating. I panicked.

I suddenly understood that I could never conquer my disease. In order to heal, I would have to accept my illness as an inner master—or in this case, an inner mistress. I had to bend my mind to it; I had to obey at whatever cost, even if it meant giving up my honorable profession. Lying there alone with bloody diarrhea, feeling hopeless and overwhelmed, I decided to start listening to my fever. There had to be a hidden meaning; some god was lurking there in the sullen revolt of my entrails. I had to surrender to my physicality. That day I laid to rest the spurious notion that my body was a separate entity from the rest of myself; I finally realized my body was not simply a beast of burden or a machine with no soul.

Being ill forced me to take stock of my genetic inheritance, the profound legacy of thousands of years of evolution that I can ignore only at my peril. I learned that humans originally ate nuts, leaves, roots, raw cereals, and fruit, and that these foods are the easiest for the organism to assimilate. Through my own body I rediscovered the history of the evolution of the species. Our bodies are products of a progressive adaptation to the environment and cannot be dissociated from their ecological niche.

My recovery, after eight years of health problems that had left me sallow, weak, and anemic, was utterly amazing. After a few weeks on a diet of natural foods,[3] I stopped losing blood, and a few months later I was no longer taking any medication. It was a second birth. I rediscovered a vitality and a joy in living that I hadn't felt since my childhood. Having spent so much time trying to quash the revolt in my body, and fully convinced I would be sick for the rest of my days, I now felt as though I had risen from the dead.

When you have suffered through a wasting illness like this, recovering your health is an indescribable experience. You plunge into life with your full being: every instant is precious. The idea of death becomes a positive presence, a stimulant to living fully and making the most of every moment. My sickness brought me back to life. Had I not been so ill, I would never have known this feeling, this physical, bodily sensation of a vigorous and enthusiastic involvement in existence. I sensed that being alive is a blessing: the essential purpose of our presence on earth is to appreciate the gift of life and to celebrate it.[4]

DEPRESSION AS INITIATION

Shattered Ideals

When we are adolescents we think everything is possible: we can become whatever we want. The realities of chance and choice, however, require us to follow a single path only. We are not omnipotent gods, and we cannot be all things at once. Life irreparably compromises us; it particularizes and individualizes us. We must say good-bye to our dreams of being heroes, good-bye to those admirable, noble causes, good-bye

---

3. This diet was suggested by Dr. Blanche-Neige Royer Bach-Thuet, a Montreal naturopath to whom I am extremely grateful.

4. In the interests of accuracy, I should add that since the time this was written, my illness has flared up again on several occasions. Each time, however, recovering my health has involved the same process: a return to the body and nature.

to our rebellious idealism, good-bye to the whole shebang. The milk is spilt; we must get on with our lives.

Life mutilates our ideals terribly, as if in the dark embrace of our material existence a secret lies waiting to be discovered. This secret seems to be revealed through suffering. Whether they are caused by accidents, solitude, or self-confrontation, these mutilations feel like we are being expelled from paradise; we find ourselves cast out from the womb of our earthly mother. Where are you, mother of infinite goodness and gentleness? What has become of the soft, tropical life in the womb? Why must we go through life always on the defensive? When we undergo a mutilating experience we suddenly are faced with a brutal realization: we are not the darlings of the gods, we are not divine, we have not been chosen or elected above all others, we are not what we imagined ourselves to be. Fate dares to strike her favorite sons. With revolt in our hearts at being abandoned by heaven, we have to resign ourselves to living with our human imperfections.

The following is a dream that Gus, a man of forty, had just after his wife threw him out of their home:

I was in a bedroom, sitting on a bed with my brother-in-law. He handed me a plastic garbage bag in which I found a present I had given to my wife. It was a sculpture I was particularly fond of; it looked like a castle. The castle had been smashed to bits, though, and I was perplexed. I wondered if I should try to glue it together again.

The castle represented Gus's ideals, broken into pieces by the harshness of life. Gus was suffering terribly from the breakup of his family, the family he had cherished perhaps more in his imagination than in his actions. He had tremendous trouble accepting that fate could destroy what had once been perfect, especially because he himself had gone through a difficult childhood with parents who had separated.

For many men, a shipwreck like Gus's is a one-way trip; these men become cynical, their boats are shipping water, they will never make it back to the land. Depression can serve as a springboard to change for them, though, providing they accept the depression and experience it fully, in their entrails. Men must acknowledge the necessity of depression and lay to rest their impossible desires.

Falling Pretty Goddamned Fast

"I feel like somebody threw me off the top of the Empire State Building and I'm falling pretty goddamned fast!" This is what one of my friends said when he arrived at my office in a panic while I was on my lunch hour. He was in tears, unable to understand what was happening to him. After several months of overwork he had collapsed. He had accumulated thousands of dollars of debt in just a few weeks and now he could hardly place one foot ahead of the other; he was so frightened and depressed he could hardly bring himself to leave his house.

Our society suffers from the scourges of anxiety and depression. These days, to make it sound less frightening, we call depression burnout. Over the years I have seen my relatives, patients, and friends fall one by one into the black abyss; they become suddenly infected with a lack of energy. Usually full of vim and vigor, one day they find themselves incapable of going to work because they're having dizzy spells. They are confronted by emptiness, bleakness, and need.

Everybody thinks it's just a rough period that they must go through, but it keeps dragging on. So they rebel. Telling them that they're probably going through a change for the better, that they're feeling down because they haven't respected their own true nature, is finally a waste of breath. They may appear to agree, but deep down they don't believe a word of it. As soon as they've recovered a bit of energy, they pathetically try to pull themselves together and push themselves to work even harder; then a few months later, they fall into even worse depression. They suffer from exhaustion, repeated colds, persistent bronchitis. They fight desperately against their own nature to avoid losing face, to prove they can handle it. If only they knew that the depression they fear so much is actually a lot less serious than what they are already suffering from!

They refuse to change their behavior in the world they usually operate in; they resist lessening their daily heroics. They fear the characters they glimpse in their nightmares: the simpleton, the cripple, the retardate, the delinquent. They do not understand that the creative soul always appears in its deformed version. Hephaistos, the Greek god of creativity, was so ugly that when he was born his mother Hera threw him down from Mount Olympus.

What is novel and creative in us often presents itself in a repulsive form, in a form rejected by the family and society. This is eloquently symbolized in myth by Hera's gesture. Hephaistos, the creator, is a loner. He does not take part in life on Olympus and does not participate in the heroism of the gods and goddesses. He frightens us, and his monstrous appearance mirrors our fear. Creative depression, like death, can only be experienced by a loner. It sets him apart and particularizes him, especially when he has subscribed too fully to the ideals of society and sacrificed his own individuality.

Creativity needs chronic disorder to survive. When everything is in order, stagnation sets in. Our disorders terrify us, though. We do not believe that there can be a god—or a meaning hidden in our illnesses. I know one person suffering from an acute ulcer who was told point-blank by a specialist in psychosomatic disorders that his illness was the healthiest part of his personality: his ulcer prevented him from cultivating false ideas about himself and forced him to live according to his true nature.

Frightened of Your Own Shadow

Most people do not trust their inner resources. In fact they are usually scared of them. Even before they go into a therapist's office, most individuals already have an idea of what they should do to improve their lives. They are afraid, though—

afraid of what's inside them, afraid of their desires, afraid of their abilities.

The shadow, which shows its repulsive face in times of depression, is a part of ourselves that we consider inferior. We try to keep it hidden, like a deformed little brother we don't want anyone to see. Most of the time we get rid of it by projecting it outward, onto others. We decide that someone is a hypocrite, someone else is full of himself, or that all immigrants are lazy. These are all dimensions of ourselves that we have erased so we don't have to face up to them. We end up missing them, though, their absence impoverishes our personalities.

Why are we so frightened of our shadow? Could it be because of the failure of our beautiful dreams of grandeur and perfection? Could it be because we realize that what we have always denigrated in others is part of us too? When our fine self-image falls apart, the entire personality gets dragged down into bleakness. We discover we are not perfect. We realize our way of seeing things is relative, not absolute. We become aware of our deep internal needs: our need for others, for love, for affection and understanding. Our pseudo-independence then gives way to a painful awareness of extreme dependence. When we understand that nobody owes us anything, that we are not innocent victims but that we are responsible for what happens to us, then we also become responsible for attempting what is possible in our desires. Becoming aware of our shadow marks the end of the impossible dream of a magic, benevolent world in which all our desires can be fulfilled without costing us our lives.

In Deep Shit

The alchemists of old claimed that the primary raw material they needed for their work of transformation was a substance everyone despised and trampled underfoot. Some illustrations, in fact, depict them standing in manure. This manure has a psychological significance: the alchemists were not looking for common gold, but rather for philosophical gold, which is the product of self-investigation. The work of transforming our inner selves, then, begins when we are "in deep shit."

This reality is illustrated by one of the dreams of Michael, the homosexual, who had turned his aggression against himself because his violent, alcoholic father constantly belittled him. Michael suffered from deep despair: when he was younger he had tried several times to commit suicide. I therefore wasn't all that surprised when he reported this dream:

> *I was in the kitchen of my parents' house, arguing with my mother. Suddenly a hole opened up in the middle of the floor, and I found myself in the cellar. There I saw a monkey playing with obvious pleasure in two huge piles of shit. I was completely disgusted.*

All Michael's vitality and pleasure in life had been relegated to the unconscious; the monkey playing in the pile of shit represented his own instinctive shadow, which he had always rejected. The monkey stood in striking contrast to Michael's impeccable appearance and fine manners. Michael's overly fastidious ego had provoked a crisis. I saw this dream as a positive sign for Michael because the primary material for transformation, repugnant though it was, was certainly present in it.

Roger, the man who dreamed of the tiger, told me about another dream:

> *I had shit my pants. I was with a group of people and couldn't leave, so I had to remain seated and wait with the people around me. I finally decided to look for a washroom where I could clean myself up. I looked everywhere; I found several in various dilapidated buildings, but there was no seat on any of the toilets.*

The king has no throne to sit on. The ego has been unthroned and Roger, having lost his comfortable position, is now worried about what others will think. The decrepit buildings, in which he has to look for a place to relieve himself and get cleaned up in, represent his past, the old parts of his personality. They are the parts that he abandoned and left to return to their primitive, uncivilized state. These buildings are Roger's first glimpses of the land of the shadow: the past he left behind and the possibilities he never explored. The buildings, in their state of disrepair symbolize the back yard or back room of a personality and the irreparable disorder we try so hard to hide.[5] This is where the soul does its work, though, in the midst of shit and decay, breaking down the old elements to transform them into something new.

INNER BALANCE

The Shattered Ego

The astrophysicist Hubert Reeves said in a recent interview that we have not yet realized how great a catastrophe lies in the fact that we have finally mastered nature. There is no longer anything to oppose us. But we must have something to oppose our will, something that does not succumb to our desires. Otherwise we will go mad.

I believe that illness still remains as something that does not conform to our wishes, though. Illness is precious because we do not deliberately create it; it is an irrepressible reflex of our deepest nature. Being ill reminds us that there is an objective balance within us. Similarly, the illness of the environment reminds us of physical laws we cannot transgress with impunity. Illnesses are manifestations of otherness, of the objective existence of the world and the psyche.

The basic element in Michael's and Roger's dreams is invol-

5. For an excellent discussion of this subject, see the article by James Hillman, "La Culture et la chronicité du désordre" (Culture and Chronic Disorder"), *La Petite Revue de philosophie*, vol. 9, no. 2, (Longueuil, Que.: College Edouard-Montpetit, 1988), pp. 12–25.

untary behavior. Michael unexpectedly finds himself sur-
rounded by shit in the cellar of his parents' house, and Roger
has lost control of his sphincter muscles. These involuntary
actions symbolize the autonomous actions of the psyche.
Becoming aware of the autonomy of the unconscious is a
wrenching experience: we can no longer maintain the illusion
of power that is so dear to our ego.

Depression will last as long as the ego clings to its preten-
tions to absolute control and avoids coming to terms with its
inner partner. The individual must understand his depression:
it clearly indicates that the forces within him have mutinied;
they are serving notice to the ship's captain that although he
is navigating according to the stars—the externally accepted
ideals—he is nevertheless mistreating his crew. The psyche
demands democracy.

In the Blink of an Eye

In our world, we live more and more quickly; we do everything
in the blink of an eye. How long can a person or a civilization
go on, though, spinning in this way? The answer is apparent
in the dizziness and light-headedness experienced by the growing number of people suffering from depression. Psychology
attempts to reduce the symptoms of mental illness to a set of
personal, subjective factors; these factors in fact provide objective information about the state of health—or more precisely,
the state of illness—of our entire civilization. Mental illness is
the barometer of our society. It confronts us with an objective
equilibrium, an intelligence above and beyond our individual
comprehension that is at work in our world.

The phenomena of depression and mental illness are out of
our control. They remind us we are not the only masters in
our homes. We should acknowledge their role in saving us
from an unreal world in which everything is in our own image.
To become real as individuals, we must start listening to the
reality of what is other than ourselves. In recognizing the

substance and intelligence of what is around and within us, we ourselves gain substance and reality.

I said earlier that the father plays a fundamental role in the child's psychological structuring. In preventing his son from acting out his incestuous desire, he allows his son's interiority to develop, and blocks the fusion of his son's ego with the unconscious. Depression performs an identical function. By frustrating his ability to act, it confronts the individual with his inner workings. The ancient rituals have become internalized today: because our fathers are missing, we must cover ourselves with the ashes of depression in order to experience rebirth.

SEVEN

Breaking the Silence

HEALING

Practical psychological approaches can help us recover from depression or restore our wounded masculinity. Some of these approaches involve changes in only the individual himself, while others involve collective changes of attitude. All these approaches aim to improve men's relationships with themselves and with others.

Letting Go

What happens when we embrace our shadow? What does the narrow door of depression open onto? Where does working on ourselves lead to? When an individual's experiences have completely drained him of energy to deal with the external world, he becomes less defensive and less sensitive to what others think of him. He becomes more open to risk taking and self-affirmation. He realizes, with amazement, that instead of meeting rejection when he assumes his rightful place, he meets respect. He wonders why he spent so many years hiding his true self. In showing his shadow he moves out of the shadows.

The individual also becomes aware of the objective aspect of his fate. He realizes that he need not feel shame about growing up in poverty or having an alcoholic father. He now knows where his anger and greed come from. He becomes aware that his moodiness has a history; he understands this history and can account for it. Getting in touch with his deep, obscure motivations makes it possible for him to stop endlessly repeating the same sordid soap opera in his life. Although he is not responsible for his objective fate, he is indeed responsible for making sense of that fate.

The road to responsibility is the road to freedom. When an individual stops telling himself it's somebody else's fault, a new world opens up for him. Understanding and accepting himself will prepare him to accept the consequences of his actions. He will no longer need to beg understanding from others or to humble himself in order to obtain it.

When an individual accepts his shadow, however, he must make a permanent break with the idea of his own perfection. He must realize he will never be perfect: he will never live long enough to change everything he doesn't like about himself. He must modify his conception of change as a horizontal, linear progression. Would he really be happier if he used more self-discipline or if he owned a house? If he is not satisfied with what he is at the present moment, is he likely to be more satisfied in the distant future? Is it really so important to be some way or other, some thing or other? Would it not be preferable for him to move to a higher plane and cultivate an overall acceptance of what he really is? One of the paradoxes of change is that it often happens only when we've stopped striving for it.

Self-detachment enables the individual to gain a greater appreciation of his own existence, the people around him, and his own personality. Instead of moving him further away from life, self-detachment plunges him more deeply into it. The man who accepts his own relativity also accepts the relativity of others. In a world where he does not have to watch his every step, he can breathe more freely. When he knows his own shadow, he no longer fears that others will turn into vicious tigers and attack him. He can now take pleasure in the realization that we are all interdependent.

The great lesson to be learned from the shadow is tolerance. Discovering his own vulnerabilities makes a man more tolerant of the failings of other people in his life. Discovering his own needs for attention and understanding renders him more attentive and understanding of others. Acknowledging his own inevitable dependence enables him to acknowledge others' dependence on him. He stops feeling tyrannized by demands that are placed on him, and he also stops tyrannizing others with his own demands. He gains access to the world of gratitude because he knows that though no one owes him anything, someone gives him a hand.

The Inner Dialogue

William, a tall redheaded man with the stature of a Viking, arrives for his session feeling sad, depressed, and aggressive. That morning his girlfriend was cold and unresponsive toward him; she was in a hurry to leave for work. William is over-whelmed by negative feelings. If he remains in their grip, he will stay closed and aggressive until his girlfriend does some-thing to atone for her lack of attention. But if he sidesteps them he can enter into a dialogue with his bad mood—he can let it take symbolic form in images.

Memories of his childhood come spontaneously to the surface for William. He sees himself protesting violently be-cause he didn't want to go to school, or angry because his mother showed favoritism toward his brother. He now realizes that he has interpreted his situation with his girlfriend through the filter of the past. He has blamed her for feelings that don't belong to her; in fact those feelings are his own. He has accused his girlfriend of acting colder and more distant than she actually did.

This session didn't get rid of William's sadness—he still had to talk the problems over with his girlfriend—but it did stop

his feeling trapped in the enraged silence of his disappointment. He could function again, having gained a bit of inner
freedom. The objectifying in this session enabled him to
express his real needs to his companion rather than waste time
with angry recriminations. It also allowed him to understand
a particularly vulnerable part of his personality. His girlfriend
was not responsible for his past; he would have to learn to
console himself by himself.

We possess the wonderful possibility of seeing our feelings
in terms of images. When you think about it, this simple
ability to objectify our emotions is what makes us most
different from animals. It shows that we are not absolutely
bound to act according to the automatic responses of our
physical biology. It is a salutary factor in our evolution.

Therapy

These days psychotherapy is one of the most common meth-
ods of dealing with psychological problems. Regardless of
whether it's Jungian psychoanalysis, regular psychoanalysis, or
any other kind of therapy, though, there is no magic solution!
An individual attains psychological maturity only after working long and hard on himself. Although short-term therapy
can ease a crisis, the long-term goal of all therapy is to develop
an individual's capacity to have a spontaneous relationship
with himself and with others. It is illusory to think that a
problem that has taken years to come to a head can be
corrected in just a few months.

What kind of therapist should a man choose? A male
therapist or a female? Since our focus here is on masculine
identity, my spontaneous answer would be a man. A man's
relationship with his father may have been so badly damaged,
however—or he may have so much mistrust toward men in
general—that he would not be able to benefit from working
with a male therapist. In such a case it would be much better
to begin with a woman and then, if appropriate, work with a
man later.

But I have noticed that relatively few male therapists have worked on their own masculinity or sufficiently explored their past relationship with their own fathers. There is no point in referring male patients with identity problems to them, since these therapists will tend to view men's difficulties in the conventional terms of mother-son relationships. I therefore often refer male patients to female therapists who take an active interest in the role of men in our society. Their being women does not prevent them from hearing what men leave unspoken.

Efficient therapy must affect the world of the emotions. Unless it has an impact on the individual, in either an agreeable or disagreeable sense, therapy is simply not worth the effort. The roots of our complexes are emotional; to take advantage of the vitality locked away in these complexes, we must stir up our emotions. What makes therapy difficult, complicated, and painful is our resistance to accepting what rises up from the depths of our being.

Therapeutic procedure for the patient is not so much "doing something" as letting himself be worked on by the various souls that inhabit him. By letting what is within him float to the surface, and by increasingly giving himself up to what is within him, the individual rediscovers his center. Then he can get on with the life that should be his.

Therapy aims to explore the world of the psyche; this exploration aims to help the individual celebrate his objective nature. The goal of therapy for the patient is to establish a living relationship with himself. Therapy does not aim for perfection. It is impossible to change everything we would like to change about ourselves. Although self-improvement is important, the greatest improvement is the one that enables a person to start loving himself just as he is. Loving himself like this involves a change in attitude more than a change in behavior. Our behavior reflects what is going on inside us; when the heart changes, behavior follows.

At its best, therapy should be a process of desubjectivization, that is, a way in which an individual can shed enough light on his personal life and his own motivations to be able to see their shared universal structures. In the words of the philosopher Gabriel Marcel, "The intimate is universal." The self-detachment that therapy produces can enable an individual to get free of himself. He can plunge without fear into the multiple realities of his nature and his being, and take pleasure in the miracle of being alive and human.

Men's Groups

Individual therapy is not the only kind. Taking part in men's groups can reinforce a man's identity and self-confidence. As I indicated earlier, a men's group may act as a symbolic womb in which a second birth takes place—a masculine rebirth.

Men's groups are good at making problems seem less dramatic since the men in them are very different and the men's experiences are very similar. By sharing their experiences in a group, men emerge from the isolation of their own particular problems. The simple awareness of other men's difficulties seems to lighten the burden of individual fate. The exchanges that take place in men's groups are usually very productive.

Unfortunately there are not very many of these groups at the present time. One solution to this problem is to take the bull by the horns and organize a group with your peers. A self-help group may or may not include a professional facilitator; when there is no leader, it's better to limit the group to only a few persons.

Male Friendships

Too many men live cut off and isolated from the male community. Cultivating the friendship of other men can only be a beneficial experience for them. The fragility of masculine identity requires that these friendships be maintained over time, since identity can never be assured once and for all. A man's identity is always in danger of regressing; a man might at any time set up new barriers, cut himself off again, or retreat into his own head. His friends encourage him to be present in the world; his friends might share his sports activities, his table, or his psychological questioning.

Psychological Glasses

My experience with men's groups has convinced me that all men are more or less caught up in a one-dimensional model of masculinity without being aware of it. Reexaminations of Greek mythology, as in the work of the psychosociologist Ginette Paris[1] and the analyst James Hillman, can show us other ways of being a man. These reexaminations are not a going backwards, they are a discovery of what is eternal in the masculine qualities of the ancient gods; we can use these qualities to determine whether or not the forces we usually relegate to the shadows can help guide us in our contemporary world.

Most important of all, men must move away from rigid behavioral models and make room for the workings of their inner souls: the warrior soul, the sentimental soul, or the homosexual soul. The monotheism of Western thought has made them soulless men in the literal sense.

James Hillman talks about rediscovering the polytheistic nature of the soul. Hillman uses the concept of "psychological glasses" to describe the effects our various souls have on us. Some days we look at life through an old person's glasses, which make everything seem difficult. Other days we see it through the eyes of a teenager, and everything seems possible. Our view of things may be sad or glad, pensive or sensitive. We must learn to distinguish among our ways of seeing so that we can develop a new psychological flexibility. We may even

---

1. Ginette Paris, *Le Réveil des dieux, la découverte de soi et des autres à travers les mythes* ("The Awakening of the Gods: Discovering Oneself and Others Through Myths"), (Boucherville, Que.: Editions de Mortagne, 1981), p. 332ff. The author discusses Dionysus, Apollo, Hermes, and Zeus in the contemporary world.

reach the point where we can choose our glasses according to events. Psychological differentiation remains our surest guarantee of freedom.

Today Ares, the warrior, might visit us, but yesterday it was Hermes, the diplomat, and last week it was Apollo, god of balance and wisdom. The goddesses also visit us. Beautiful Aphrodite bathes us in sensuality; Demeter, the bountiful mother, fills us with generosity or feelings of revenge; Athena, the intellectual warrior and patron of the arts, brings us inspiration; Hera makes us heroic, and Artemis leads us off into the solitude of the forest.

All the gods and goddesses invite us to join in their dances. They can bring us joy and happiness; they can also bring us damnation. It all depends on our attitude. Each of them has his or her own mystery; each rules over some dimension of reality; each summons us to the discovery of life. Unless we know who we are dancing with, we are like puppets on a string, jerked about by invisible masters, unable to do anything about it.

Acknowledging our psychologically polytheistic selves helps us avoid monolithic attitudes and thinking. It enables us to relax about the ways we experience our masculinity, and it also frees us from thorny questions of sexual differences. The gods and goddesses call to men and women both without distinction. The polytheistic self lets us go beyond ridiculous divisions of characteristics according to gender: men must be strong and intellectual; women must be sentimental, sensitive, and vulnerable. These distinctions suggest that if a man suddenly feels fragile and close to tears, he automatically feels more feminine. Such an attitude implies a terrible contempt for women; contempt of this sort permeates and poisons our entire culture.

It is true that men must get in touch with the aggressive energies buried in their bodies. Men cannot realize a genuine awakening of their vitality, though, unless they participate fully in the world of emotions and feelings, a dimension of themselves that is constantly projected onto women (and homosexuals). Men can no longer get away with attributing to women a weakness that is actually their own. *Cinderella* and *Sleeping Beauty* are parables of man's repressed anima, of his emotional world still unawakened, scorned, subjugated, and neglected.

Vulnerability, feeling, intellect, strength, and courage do not belong exclusively to either men or women. These qualities are the common heritage of humanity. Emotion is part of all human beings. As Maurice Champagne-Gilbert states, "Men should be less concerned with conquering space or inventing major new technologies; their real challenge lies in conquering a new relationship with life, a relationship in which the values traditionally labeled as feminine are repossessed by men as existential values."[2]

Conquering our masculine identity is important because it makes us better human beings. Sexual identity provides us with a foundation, a basic way of understanding reality. Our goal must always be to attain the wholeness of life. It doesn't matter a damn if all our myths and stereotypes get lost on the way.

SELF-FATHERING

Mourning the Ideal Father and Forgiving the Real Father

Our fathers are missing. The patriarchal social system that allowed previous generations of men to stand tall and proud has been widely discredited. Initiation rites no longer exist. The hunger for a father's presence still remains in us, though. We realize we have unresolved problems of identity, but the only solution we ever get from our elders is "Grit your teeth

---

2. Maurice Champagne-Gilbert, "La Famille, survivra-t-elle?" ("Will the Family Survive?"), *Le Devoir*, Saturday, December 12, 1987, p. A-9.

and bear it; it won't last forever." They don't even know what we're talking about. To compensate for our inner emptiness, some of us choose a career our father would approve of; others are lucky enough to find substitute fathers. However we compensate, the fact remains that a deep desire for a father's recognition stays with us for a very long time.

This is a good reason to reflect upon what we expect from the father. Our desires in this regard are impossible to fulfill: what we are really looking for is recognition from an archetypal father, a father who possesses every good quality we could possibly imagine. We would like him to be an athlete and initiate us into the world of sports. We would like him to be a nature lover and teach us the secrets of the fields and forests. We would like him to be an intellectual and show us how to read and think. We would like him to be an artist and reveal to us the wonders of the imagination. We would sometimes like him to be stern and authoritarian; other times we would like him to be a friend and companion. The list of our desires is endless.

These expectations are clearly beyond the capacities of any human being to satisfy. We want more from our fathers than they can possibly give us. After all, our fathers are men, not gods. Traditional tribal initiations were not conducted by a boy's own individual father, but rather by the tribal fathers of the community. A man needs a variety of masculine models if he is to attain his own individuality.

Adult sons must be able to mourn their ideal fathers. The mourning process will teach them how to father themselves, how to fill their inner emptiness through creativity. The transition from being a son to being a man involves giving up the ideal father and giving in to the ideal itself. The challenge for men with missing fathers is to themselves become the fathers they lacked. It doesn't matter if they father real children or cultural artifacts. In the area of psychology, we might say that we can really only give what we have never received. Therein lies the mystery of human creativity.

The psychoanalyst Stephen Shapiro states: "We have noted that accepting the suffering that comes with ending the illusion of perfect care is what enables a man to emerge into the gap left by the absent father and to fill it up with his own presence."[3] The void left in us by our missing fathers itself gives us the opportunity to become men—on condition we stop our eternal complaining and provide ourselves with the care and attention we never received from our fathers.

It is difficult for us to forgive our fathers for what we see as their cowardice in betraying and deserting us, yet most of the time they did what they could. They protected us, many of them were good breadwinners, and often they made real sacrifices to give us an education. Still, they were not available to talk to us and guide us. That's the way it was: nothing can change it now. Certainly there were failings. Certainly they left us clinging to mommy's skirts for too long, but the time has come to forgive all this. "My father's silence is a temptation to rage and an opportunity to speak. The choice is mine."[4]

To quote Shapiro yet again, "The contemporary denigration of fatherhood and authority is compounded of the mythology of an absent, idealized daddy, a bitter clinging to feelings of betrayal and abandonment, a refusal to suffer the present situation, and an infantile inclination to rebel against one's own commitments."[5] Our mythological vision of the absent father results from a negative father complex that lets us see only our fathers' failings and prevents us from acknowledging their good sides. It is clearly a difficult task to put aside our suffering and open ourselves up to the love our parents had for us. It is almost painful for us to realize how generous they have been to us and how many sacrifices they have made on our behalf. We don't like to be reminded of their affection, and we often refuse to recognize it in their silence.

3. Shapiro, *Manhood*, p. 100.
4. Ibid., p. 96.
5. Ibid., p. 99.

How to Heal the Wounded Father in Ourselves

How can a man heal the wounded father within him and move beyond the anger he feels toward his real father? The psychologist Samuel Osherson suggests an in-depth exploration of the father's past as a way of understanding his suffering and developing an empathy that may help his son forgive him. Osherson also speaks of the necessity of renouncing the myth of the ideal father and being prepared to endure the solitude that results from this.

Osherson discusses the benefits of imaginary dialogues with a father who is dead or far away. These dialogues may take the form of letters or psychological role-playing. They can function as forums for expressing unresolved feelings of rage, anger, and disappointment. These feelings can then be objectified and more fully accepted. This process can help a man escape from the prison of his unconscious and transform his current negative feelings into memories.

Breaking the Father's Silence

Our fathers' silence has become our own. Although we have been inducted into the mafia of hereditary silence, our awareness of the suffering this silence has caused us (and our fathers) should discourage us from passing it on to our own sons. The challenge facing men today is to break this long tradition of male silence. It is perhaps the most truly revolutionary act we can ever accomplish.

Those of us who can should start dialogues with our real fathers, despite the fear, frustration, disappointment, or rejection this may lead to. We must fight against falling into the same silence our fathers did; we must try to bridge the gap that separates us from our fathers. By bridging this gap, we can begin to heal the terrible division between the abstract, disincarnated minds of men and an increasingly cruel world. The time has come to talk of our vulnerability, our deep needs, our internal violence. The time has come for us to proclaim our visions. The time has come for us to share and show ourselves as we actually are, to open ourselves up and become real in the eyes of the people around us. The time has finally come for us to speak.

CONCLUSION

A man is born three times in his life. He is born of his mother, he is born of his father, and finally he is born of his own deep self. This last is the birth of his individuality. Christ referred to it when he said that he knew neither his father nor his mother, even though his parents were in the crowd that had come to hear him speak. Men's mourning for the unrealistic expectations they had of their fathers, and the solitude this mourning imposes upon them, are experiences that liberate them. Their suffering serves as an initiatory mutilation; it forces them to confront the reality of the objective world: the whole universe becomes their new home.

It is more and more urgent that we end our deadly silence about the disintegration of the family, the exploitation of the Third World by the developed countries, the arms race, and the pollution that is destroying us. We must shout our fear from the rooftops and make sure that governments finally hear our voices.

Unless we recover our sense of ourselves as integral parts of humanity and of the entire universe—animal, mineral, and vegetable—we shall simply not survive. Each of us is afflicted with the Fisher King's wound and we each have a duty to heal it. Fine theories are of no use. The time has come for us to look ourselves in the face and decide whether or not we want to go on. The decision is ours. If we do not break the silence, we will not survive.

I am convinced that men's true transformation and healing will necessarily involve their rediscovery of their *psychological and physical spontaneity*. Their recovery of their vitality must spring from a natural religion, a religion based on cultivating a simple sense of oneness with the world. In the words of Frédéric Back, who won an Oscar for his film *The Man Who Planted Trees*, "We are creatures of the earth and the earth is the raw material for our happiness."

In order to change we must regain possession of our emotions and the organic sensations of our bodies. Our transformation finally will come from a recognition of the wisdom of our instincts. We must learn again to trust the animal within us. We must give up our arrogant illusions of control that lead to the oppression of every creature on earth.

Let me close by paraphrasing a Native American poem: Stones need neither sun nor water to exist; plants need stones, water, soil, and sun to live; animals need plants, stones, water, soil, and sun to survive; human beings need animals, plants, stones, water, soil, and sun to go on living; humans are therefore the most dependent creatures of all.

BIBLIOGRAPHY

Anquetil, Gilles. "Mais où sont les pères-à-penser?" *Autrement* (Pères et fils), no. 61. Paris, June 1984.

Apollon, Willy. "La Masculinité en butte à la paternité." *Un Amour de père*. Montreal: Saint-Martin, 1988.

Bernstein, Jerome, S. "The Decline of Masculine Rites of Passage in Our Culture: The Impact on Masculine Individuation." *Betwixt and Between: Patterns of Masculine and Feminine Initiation*. LaSalle, Ill.: Open Court, 1987.

Bigras, Julien. *Le Psychanalyste nu*, coll. Reponses. Paris: Robert Laffont, 1979.

Biller, Henry B. "Fatherhood: Implications for Child and Adult Development." *Handbook of Developmental Psychology*. Englewood Cliffs, N.J.: Prentice Hall, 1982.

Bly, Robert. "The Erosion of Male Confidence." *Betwixt and Between: Patterns of Masculine and Feminine Initiation*. LaSalle, Ill.: Open Court, 1987.

―――. "What Men Really Want: A New Age Interview with Robert Bly by Keith Thompson." *New Age Journal*. May 1982, pp. 31–51.

―――. "Initiations masculines contemporaines." *Guides-Ressources*, vol. 4, no. 2. Montreal, November/December 1988. (Translated from the English by Jean-Guy Girouard.)

Campbell, Joseph, and Moyers, Bill. *The Power of Myth*. New York: Doubleday, 1988.

Castaneda, Carlos. *The Fire from Within*. New York: Simon and Schuster, 1984.

Chabot, Marc. "Le Père des pays d'en-haut." *Un Amour de père*. Montreal: Saint-Martin, 1988.

Champagne-Gilbert, Maurice. "La Famille survivra-elle?" *Le Devoir.* Saturday, December 12, 1987, p. A-9.

Delaisi de Parseval, Geneviève. "De l'identique à l'identité" (Interview). *Autrement* (Pères et fils), no. 61. Paris, June 1984.

Embareck, Michel. "Sagas en baskets." *Autrement* (Pères et fils), no. 61. Paris, June 1984.

Falconnet, G., and Lefaucheur, N. *La Fabrication des mâles,* coll. Points, séries Actuels, no. A17. Paris: Seuil, 1975.

Fromm, E., and Maccoby, M. *Social Character in a Mexican Village.* Englewood Cliffs, N.J.: Prentice Hall, 1970.

Gustafson, Fred R. "Fathers, Sons and Brotherhood." *Betwixt and Between: Patterns of Masculine and Feminine Initiation.* LaSalle, Ill.: Open Court, 1987.

Guy-Gillet, Geneviève. "Le Roi-Pêcheur: Jung parle de son père." *Le Père en question,* Jungian Psychology Journals, no. 35. Paris: Fourth Trimester, 1982.

Health and Welfare Canada, *Alcohol in Canada, a National Perspective,* Second Revised Edition. Ottawa, 1984.

Henderson, Joseph L. *Thresholds of Initiation.* Middletown, Conn.: Wesleyan University Press, 1967.

Hillman, James. *L'amour de la guerre,* Journals of the C. G. Jung Circle of Montreal. Montreal, May 1987.

———. "La Culture et la chronicité du désordre." *La Petite Revue de philosophie,* vol. 9, no. 2. Longueuil, Que.: Collège Edouard-Montpetit, 1988.

Hopcke, Robert H. *Jung, Jungians and Homosexuality.* Boston: Shambhala Publications, 1989.

Johnson, Robert A. *He: Understanding Masculine Psychology,* coll. Perennial Library, no. P415. New York: Harper and Row, 1977.

Jung, Carl Gustav. *Psychological Types,* Collected Works, vol. 6, Bollingen Series XX, Second Edition. Princeton, N.J.: Princeton University Press, 1967.

———. *Métamorphoses de l'âme et ses symboles.* Georg et Cie, Geneva: Librairie de l'Université, 1967.

———. *Psychology and Alchemy,* Collected Works, vol. 12, Bollingen Series XX, Second Edition. Princeton, N.J.: Princeton University Press, 1968.

———. *Psychology and Religion: West and East,* Collected Works, vol.

11, Bollingen Series XX. Princeton, N.J.: Princeton University Press, 1956.

―――. *Symbols of Transformation: an Analysis of the Prelude to a Case of Schizophrenia*, Collected Works, vol. 5, Bollingen Series XX, Second Edition. Princeton, N.J.: Princeton University Press, 1967.

Kinsey, Alfred, Pomeroy, Wardell, and Martin, Clyde E. *Sexual Behavior in the Human Male*. Philadelphia: W. B. Saunders, 1948.

Kohut, Heinz. *Le Soi*, coll. Le Fil Rouge. Paris: Presses Universitaires de France, 1974.

Krishnamurti, J. "The Only Revolution." *The Second Krishnamurti Reader*, published under the direction of Mary Lutyens. Penguin Books, 1973.

―――. "The Urgency of Change." *The Second Krishnamurti Reader*, published under the direction of Mary Lutyens. Penguin Books, 1973.

Laplanche, Jean, and Pontalis, J.-B. *Vocabulaire de la psychanalyse*. Paris: Presses Universitaires de France, 1967.

Larousse Library. *New Larousse Encyclopedia of Mythology*. New York: Hawlyn, 1959.

Lasch, Christopher. *The Culture of Narcissism: American Life in an Age of Diminishing Expectations*. New York: Warner Books, 1979.

―――. *The Minimal Self: Psychic Survival in Troubled Times*. New York and London: W. W. Norton, 1984.

Le Clerc, Annie. *Hommes et femmes*, coll. Le Livre de Poche, no 6150. Paris: Grasset, 1985.

Martini Field, Tiffany, and Widmayer, Susan M. "Motherhood." *Handbook of Developmental Psychology*. Englewood Cliffs, N.J.: Prentice Hall, 1982.

Monbourquette, Jean. "Grandeurs et misères de la relation père-fils, essai de psychologie archétypale de la rencontre du père et du fils." *Un Amour de père*. Montreal: Saint-Martin, 1988.

Monick, Eugene. *Phallos: Sacred Image of the Masculine*. Toronto: Inner City Books, 1987.

O'Neil, Huguette. "Santé mentale: les hommes, ces grands oubliès. . . ." *L'Actulité médicale*, May 11, 1988.

Olivier, Christiane. "Pères empêchés." *Autrement* (Pères et fils), no. 61. Paris, June 1984.

Osherson, Samuel. *Finding Our Fathers, the Unfinished Business of Manhood*. New York: Free Press, 1986.

Paris, Ginette. *La Renaissance d'Aphrodite.* Montreal: Boréal Express, 1985.

——. "Le Masque de Dionysos," conference at the C. G. Jung Circle of Montreal, May 13, 1988. (Personal notes).

——. *Le Réveil des dieux, la découverte de soi et des autres à travers les mythes.* Boucherville, Que.: Ed. de Mortagne, 1981.

Philippe, Alain. *Suicide: évolution actuelle.* Paris: Interforum, 1988.

Robert, Paul. *Le petit Robert 1,* alphabetical and analogical dictionary of the French language. Paris: Société du Nouveau Littré, 1978.

Sandner, Donald. "The Split Shadow and the Father-Son Relationship." *Betwixt and Between: Patterns of Masculine and Feminine Initiation.* LaSalle, Ill.: Open Court, 1987.

Sartorius, Bernard. "Les Archétypes du masculin," conference and seminar at the C. G. Jung Circle of Montreal, May 1986.

Shapiro, Stephen A. *Manhood, a New Definition.* New York: G. P. Putman's Sons, 1984.

Shepherd Look, Dee L. "Sex Differentiation and the Development of Sex Roles." *Handbook of Developmental Psychology.* Englewood Cliffs, N.J.: Prentice Hall, 1982.

Stevens, Anthony. *Archetypes, a Natural History of the Self.* New York: William Morrow, 1982.

Turner, Victor. "Betwixt and Between: The Liminal Period in Rites of Passage." *Betwixt and Between: Patterns of Masculine and Feminine Initiation,* published under the direction of Louise Carus Madhi, Steven Foster, and Meredith Little. LaSalle, Ill.: Open Court, 1987.

Von Franz, Marie-Louise. *Puer Aeternus: the Problem of the Puer Aeternus.* Zurich and New York: Spring Publications, 1970.

OTHER C. G. JUNG FOUNDATION BOOKS FROM SHAMBHALA PUBLICATIONS

Closeness in Personal and Professional Relationships, edited by
Harry A. Wilmer. Foreword by Maya Angelou.

Cross-Currents of Jungian Thought: An Annotated Bibliography,
by Donald R. Dyer.

*Dreams, by Marie-Louise von Franz.

*Ego and Archetype: Individuation and the Religious Function of the
Psyche,* by Edward F. Edinger.

The Female Ancestors of Christ, by Ann Belford Ulanov.

The Feminine in Fairy Tales, Revised Edition,
by Marie-Louise von Franz.

**From Freud to Jung: A Comparative Study of the Psychology of
the Unconscious,* by Liliane Frey-Rohn. Foreword by
Robert Hinshaw.

Gathering the Light: A Psychology of Meditation,
by V. Walter Odajnyk.

The Golden Ass of Apuleius: The Liberation of the Feminine in Man,
by Marie-Louise von Franz.

A Guided Tour of the Collected Works *of C. G. Jung,*
by Robert H. Hopcke. Foreword by Aryeh Maidenbaum.

In Her Image: The Unhealed Daughter's Search for Her Mother,
by Kathie Carlson.

*The Inner Child in Dreams, by Kathrin Asper.

The Inner Lover, by Valerie Harms.

Knowing Woman: A Feminine Psychology,
by Irene Claremont de Castillejo.

Lingering Shadows: Jungians, Freudians, and Anti-Semitism, edited
by Aryeh Maidenbaum and Stephen A. Martin.

(continued on next page)

Masculinity: Identity, Conflict, and Transformation,
by Warren Steinberg.

The Old Wise Woman: A Study of Active Imagination,
by Rix Weaver. Introduction by C. A. Meier.

Power and Politics: The Psychology of Soviet-American Partnership,
by Jerome S. Bernstein. Forewords by Senator Claiborne Pell
and Edward C. Whitmont, M.D.

*Psyche and Matter, by Marie-Louise von Franz.

*Psychotherapy, by Marie-Louise von Franz.

The Way of All Women, by M. Esther Harding. Introduction by
C. G. Jung.

The Wisdom of the Dream: The World of C. G. Jung,
by Stephen Segaller and Merrill Berger.

*Witches, Ogres, and the Devil's Daughter: Encounters with Evil in
Fairy Tales,* by Mario Jacoby, Verena Kast, and Ingrid Riedel.

---

*Published in association with Daimon Verlag, Einsiedeln, Switzerland.